Our Upland:

Commerce, Connections and Community In the Metaverse

Interviews, Tidbits, and Journal Prompts on Friendships, Making Money, and the Future

BY

INTERNATIONAL BEST-SELLING AUTHOR

Olivia Whiteman

and

Joe Hernandez

Credits:
Author: Olivia Whiteman, Joe Hernandez
Cover Art: DeSjaak
ISBN: 9798358501287
Printed in the United States
First U.S Edition: October 2023

Upland is an **NFT** real-estate game in the Metaverse with properties mapped to the real world. Not familiar with the Metaverse? This bestseller is a must read.

Available on Amazon.com: Navigating the Metaverse: A Guide to Limitless Possibilities in a Web 3.0 World: 9781119898993

amazon.com/Navigating-Metaverse-Guide-Limitless-Possibilities/dp/1119898994

Acknowledgements

We want to give special thanks to Tammy Revard for inviting Olivia to join her at the Upland Genesis Week event and for sharing with everyone at a session that she was from Upland which caused Joe Hernandez to come and say hello to her, as he lived near Upland.

We also want to extend gratitude to Morecheese for her kindness during the Upland party and sharing information with Olivia which helped her create this book.

A special thank-you also goes out to Shaktilyn for being generous with names of people who may be interested in participating in this book.

Of course, a special thanks to all the members who contributed a submission to the book.

Lastly, we want to express a heartfelt thanks to all the people who spread the word about the cover art contest and to all who submitted an entry. Although we could choose only one cover, you are all much appreciated.

Forward: Dirk Leuth, Uplandme, Inc.

The metaverse in general is one of the most exciting and talked-about technologies of the 21st century. It has the potential to revolutionize the way we interact with the world around us and to create new opportunities for socializing, fun, and economic prosperity.

As the co-founder of Upland, I'm often approached by people with new ideas, services, or books and articles to share. Sometimes they catch my eye, sometimes they don't. But when Joe Hernandez approached me about "Our Upland," I was immediately intrigued because it gives such a wonderful insight into the soul of Upland aka its community, and the metaverse we're all building together.

Upland's community joins and stays in the metaverse for different reasons. On a higher level you can categorize into the following five pillars why people join and how Upland will contribute to how the metaverse will transform our lives in the years and decades to come (note: only the first three are Upland's current focus):

Socializing: Uplanders can connect with each other, regardless of their physical location. They are able to meet up with friends and family, make new friends with like-minded interested people independent of their real-life status, language etc. engage with each other, build something, join live events, and eventually attend concerts and sports happenings and maybe go on virtual vacations together.

Entertainment: Upland opens up a new world of entertainment possibilities. Uplanders can play the mother of all games, the property trading game, but also race cars, and go on treasure hunts. Thanks to our third-party developer platform more games and experiences have already been launched that use an Uplander's assets and identity with many more to come. And in the near future, there will also be the possibility that Uplanders with no coding experience can create their own content.

Commerce: Upland creates a new market for goods and services. Via metaventures Uplanders can sell products and services to people all over the world, and not just via virtual money but also for real money by selling their digital assets for fiat currency.

Education: Not here yet but we also see that the metaverse will revolutionize education. Students will be able to learn in immersive virtual environments that are more engaging and interactive than traditional classrooms. They will also be able to collaborate with students from all over the world.

Work: And finally in the future, Uplanders will create new opportunities for remote work and collaboration by using tools from Upland or development partners. Employees will be able to work from anywhere in the world, and they will be able to interact with each other in real-time in virtual workspaces.

Back to the book: It was a concept that ultimately drew me in. A book about Upland through the eyes of Upland players. Welcome to *"Our Upland: Commerce, Connections and Community in the Metaverse,"* a book that celebrates the extraordinary world of Upland and the boundless possibilities it offers. Within these pages, authors Olivia Whiteman and Joe Hernandez have crafted a captivating journey that will inspire and uplift both seasoned gamers and newcomers alike.

This book illustrates how Upland stands out in the vast metaverse landscape as a shining beacon of community and connection. For your convenience, the book is divided into four sections.

Section 1 brings you the heart and soul of the game through insightful interviews with its players. Their stories of positivity, enthusiasm, and success are a testament to the power of human connections in the digital realm. As you immerse yourself in their experiences, you'll discover that Upland is not merely a game but a platform that fosters lasting relationships and personal growth.

Section 2 is a treasure trove of knowledge and wisdom. From expert strategies to historical tidbits, the authors have curated essential insights that will guide you on your journey through Upland. Moreover, the inclusion of journal prompts speaks to the belief in the transformative power of self-reflection.

Navigating a new gaming universe can sometimes be overwhelming, but fear not! Section 3 provides a comprehensive glossary that will make you feel like a seasoned pro in no time. Acquiring the unique lingo of Upland is the first step to fully immersing oneself in its magic, and this handy guide will pave the way for an enriching and immersive experience.

Finally, in Section 4, we introduce you to the team behind this remarkable venture. Knowing the people and principles that drive Upland makes the journey even more meaningful. It's the dedication to good values and a vision of profit and fun that keeps players invested and excited to share the game with others.

As you embark on this journey through "Our Upland," I hope you'll be filled with inspiration, joy, and a deep sense of belonging. May it encourage you to forge lasting connections, embrace personal growth, and become a part of something greater than yourself. Upland is not just a game; it's a canvas where dreams take flight and friendships are forged. So, let us join hands and venture forth into the metaverse, for the possibilities are as limitless as the stars above.

See you in Upland!

Message From Co-Author Olivia Whiteman

In June of 2022, my friend, Tammy, invited me to join her in Las Vegas for Genesis Week. Little did I know that it would be GREAT!!!! Here is why. The goal of Genesis Week is to celebrate the growth and progress of the Upland game, meet members of the community, and hear from the company behind it, Uplandme, Inc.

From the moment my friend and I stood in line to get our admission badges, I noticed how friendly the people around us were, and felt energy and excitement from everyone. Conversations started easily, and my knowledge about Upland increased in an important way. I learned that Upland is a property trading game in the metaverse, and that people join the game for an opportunity to build an empire.

Many people liken the Upland game to the game Monopoly. In Monopoly, you buy and sell properties even though there is no actual exchange of money worth any value outside of the game. You can land in jail (you can also go to jail in Upland if you get caught doing something against the rules). You have fun playing with other players and when you finish a game, the game is over. The Upland game never ends unless you want it to, and the virtual proprieties and other objects you collect can end up being worth money in the same way collecting baseball cards can.

I live in New York and had indicated this when I registered for the Upland app. At the event, there was a delay in the doors opening. This was a good thing, as while waiting to get in, we were informed by a more seasoned player, that it would benefit us to get to Las Vegas within the game to take advantage of bonuses being given to all attendees. I did not realize that even though I was in Las Vegas literally, I needed to be in Las Vegas in the metaverse as well. I opened the app on my phone and realized that I did not know how to transport myself from one city to another. A kind soul showed me how and I quickly realized that although it is a digital world in its own metaverse, it still takes its clues from the real world, and you actually have to travel on a bus, train, or plane, to venture from city to city.

The beautiful point I took away from this interaction and others is that you do not have to know what you are doing to succeed. People in this community share their knowledge, guide you on how to have fun, understand how to make money, and enjoy for themselves the opportunity for commerce and friendships that Upland provides. It is this point that makes me want to emphasize; do not worry that you do not know how to play the game. You will learn. People are eager to have you join the community.

In addition to friendliness, I noticed older people over sixty were talking to people who were in their twenties. People from Portugal were talking to people from Australia, United Kingdom, United States, and Canada. I don't know what other countries people came from, but there was diversity among all who had converged in real life in Las Vegas, Nevada. It became clear, in my opinion, that Upland is all about community, a view I quickly realized was shared by too many people to count. I loved that that the game was bonding people together.

As I learned more about the game and the people who contributed and connected with the game, it became clear what makes Upland so interesting to newcomers that they want to learn more about the game, and why seasoned player stay. It is because Upland is not merely a game or a community. It is a chance to create a monetary future—and I am talking about real money. Putting your money in a bank you are lucky to get 2% back on your investment. Why not get more if you can? The Upland game provides real value. You have the potential to generate real-world income through renting out your virtual properties or participating in in-game events that offer rewards with monetary value. I also learned that working with others enables players to create more impact and revenue for everyone in their groups.

It didn't take long for me to grasp the essence of Upland as a game that offered opportunities to create value for yourself.

While at the event, I met people who had invested hundreds to thousands of dollars in Upland. Since the writing of this book, I heard of one person who invested more than one million US dollars! Like all investments, some people make money, some lose, and some stay exactly where they started.

One thing that was very evident was that Upland was about far more than mere transactions of virtual properties. It was about creating shared experiences, offering support, and fostering personal growth and wealth together.

Motivated by this newfound understanding, I sought out and interviewed a range of community members, from novices to veterans, to gain insight into their motivations for joining Upland, their unique contributions, and their visionary perspectives on its future.

By the time I left the conference, I decided to write a book introducing the extraordinary individuals I had encountered. My hope was that readers like you would come to appreciate the incredible nature of this community and feel inspired to join them in their pursuit of connection, commerce, and community.

I extend an invitation to you to learn more about this community. Read their stories and delve into their experiences. More importantly, engage with fellow members in the Upland game. You do not have to attend an event to meet them. The Upland game has a chat feature.

Lastly, be sure to check out the section dedicated to the founders of Upland, as it provides an opportunity to learn more about the visionaries behind this remarkable game and community.

In my view, Upland is not merely a game. It extends far beyond financial gains—it lies in the connections we make, the knowledge we share, and the profound impact we can have on each other's lives in the metaverse and in real-life.

In closing, I want to acknowledge and thank Joe Hernandez for co-authoring this book with me, helping me connect with members of the Upland community, filling me in on gaps in my knowledge, and on getting me started with Upland. Without him, this book would not have materialized.

Message From Co- Author Joe Hernandez

I met my amazing co-author out in Las Vegas at the Light it Upland Awards Party held by Upland for Genesis Week. It was extremely serendipitous that two people from opposite coasts with such different backgrounds and interests were able to connect and now collaborate. This book is about community, and we are a great example of how the metaverse, and games can bring such differing people together.

I showed up very late to my hotel on the first night of the event June 9 nearly 3 AM so technically June 10. True to Vegas never shutting down, I had to wait in a 50-person line to check in. I was exhausted as I had just become a grandfather for the first time and was drained physically and emotionally. I had spent the drive on a three-way call via the Discord app working on Blender, a 3-D modeling software, with my partner in an outdoor decor metaventure and another fellow artist. As I finally sat down on my bed, I was excited but felt a little uncertainty. This was the first time I had ever attended anything like this. I remember telling my daughter when I bought tickets that I had gone "full gamer nerd," and that I was going to a MeetUp in Las Vegas for that game I play Upland. Her response… "Nooooo… wow you are a super dork now!" Don't you just love how supportive kids can be? (lol).

At this point in my gaming journey, I had been part of Upland for a little over a year. I was excited to meet some people in person that I had developed relationships with through the game, more specifically Discord. (If you are not familiar with Discord, look for my chapter at the end of the book on the topic).

I woke up after a few hours of sleep and worked my way out into the blazing Vegas sun. I had stayed in the hotel across the street but as anyone knows in Vegas a short walk can be very punishing. As I made my way to the hotel conference rooms area, I was greeted by a smiling face saying, "Hey man how's it going? Are you here for the Upland thing?" I responded, "Yes." I was happy to be in the right place and have such a warm and friendly welcome. I asked this player who he was, and he informed me, Rob, also known as the Agency. I asked if he could direct me up to where I needed to go and he said, let me join you. There is a line. Let's get in line." When we got in line there were about 75 people ahead of us and I could see the excitement and wandering eyes. The first person who came to approach us after we said hello to our nearest neighbors in line, a gentleman who introduced himself as YK2012 . He had a funny looking hat on with Lama ears… he generously offered us a POAP which is an NFT that you earn by attending events in real life. I had heard of these and had collected a couple, so I was very excited about it. He asked us where we were from. Rob answered, "Colorado," and I answered Los Angeles. We asked him and he responded, "Israel." All of a sudden, my four-hour trip from Los Angeles seemed like peanuts. That's when I really had a realization about how important this game was to certain people. This man standing in front of me had spent thousands of dollars to travel to meet up with fellow players and network. And that is exactly what he did, he immediately moved on to the next person in line and made his introductions and gifted them a POAP too.

As I am not a very proficient networker and as we made our way into the event, I recognized and went to introduce myself to the few people I had made connections with on Discord. Luckily one of my favorite people (Morecheese, you will learn more about her soon) invited me to join her and her husband at their table. Rob was very popular and was asked to sit at multiple tables and we ended up sitting at tables right next to each other. The food was great. The presentation was informative and not too long. They did a live city release – which is where players rush into a city to mint (buy) properties. They did this live city release in Las Vegas, the city where they were holding the event. It was rather exciting, but I must admit I minted less properties during this event than in any other prior city release due to the environment and just watching all of the other people and the excitement going on. At this event we got to hear presentations from other players who had created groups that were small software development groups and designed layer 2 Applications or games that worked with Upland. (More on this in another chapter).

Near the end of the event there was an open question session and one of the attendees mentioned she was from Upland California (you will learn more about her as well). I was immediately intrigued because that is the city, I was born in. After the event ended, I approached this woman and asked her where she lived in Upland as I was familiar with the area. She let me know that she had just moved there during the pandemic but loved it. That's when I was fortunate enough to meet my amazing co-author, Olivia Whiteman. She confidently introduced herself and said that she was new to the game and had really come to support her friend which I love and admire. She told me she was an author and I asked about her books. Without delay she reached into her bag and said - here take a look. That was when I first saw her writing. It was a compilation book about fathers called, "Honoring Dad Every Day." After thumbing through it I said this is awesome. I really like it, she responded immediately, "It's only $10 and you should buy one." Impressed by her candor and being that Father's Day was only a week away I thought why not, I'd love to support this confident woman and get my father a gift for Father's Day at the same time. So that's exactly what I did.

After that event I went back to my hotel and socialized with a few people on the way. I was offered an Uber ride by an awesome player named, "themetaversr." I remember thinking on the ride to my hotel about how kind this was and what a cool community I had become a part of. At the hotel I read part of the book and got some rest before the next event, which was the award show, which was taking place at an awesome event center, Illuminarium, nearby. There were shuttles provided from the hotel that the presentation event was held at. As I came downstairs and attempted to get an Uber over to the shuttles, I realized that my application for Uber had not been used in quite some time and I was unable to update it in time. Luckily, I had exchanged numbers with Rob, and he helped to direct me to the shuttle. That was hard, if you haven't been to Las Vegas before, each hotel is huge and finding areas within it can be very difficult. Ultimately, Rob asked the bus driver to hold and wait while he ran to find me. And he literally did run! He came up sweating and said, "thank God, I found you follow me!" We rushed to the shuttle, and again I was shocked at the kindness and generosity of this newfound friend and fellow player who I had just met that very same day. The awards event was amazing. There were floor to ceiling projections, lots of people, cocktails and hors d'oeuvres.

It was there that I ran into my co-author again. She explained to me that she was rather shy and was not really feeling very comfortable at this part of the event. She said she just wanted to go back to her hotel but would not leave her friend alone, again something I admire. I encouraged her to stay and enjoy herself, but she said she didn't drink and didn't really know anybody, so I definitely felt for her. As I sat there and thought about good excuses for her to stay, I realized and told her that she was standing in a room full of people who had come from all over the world for the love of a game. Some of these people had spent hundreds of thousands of US dollars investing in this game and believed in its future. I said to her, "You have your next book standing in this room." She responded, "You know what I think you're right, but I don't know. I really don't know anybody and I'm kind of shy. "I offered to take her around and introduce her to some of the bigger players and explain the idea to them. She accepted and we began to introduce her and the concept to some of the people. By the time we got to the fourth person (Morecheese) Olivia looked at me in the middle of the conversation and said, "I think I've got this." And she did. I went to go schmooze with other players and watch the awards and other things and she did her thing and connected with many more players there. At the end of the event, we exchanged numbers, and I told her how excited I was to read her new book and wished her lots of success. To my surprise and delight a few weeks later she reached out to me via text saying, hey you said you were an artist I really appreciate what you did in Las Vegas to help me get going, would you like to design the cover for my book?

I immediately said yes and was very happy and honored to be part of this project that would hopefully help to promote and educate people about this new game and metaverse that I had become a part of. I sent her my design very quickly after, she thanked me and said she would be sending it to Upland for approval shortly and would get back to me.

Being very excited about the prospect of the book and my design being on the cover, I followed it up a few weeks later. She responded that she had not quite finished, and she would let me know soon. Being the curious and relentless individual I am, I followed up again a few weeks later. This time she said how about we have a telephone call. And that's what we did. It was a very long conversation, nearly three hours, and at the end of the call she paused for a moment and then said, "You know I really like the way you think, and I think we could work well together. Would you consider being my co-author on this book? As I picked up my jaw from the floor, I immediately said, yes. Thank you. I would be honored! And so here we are. I am writing my introduction to a book co-authored by an international bestseller all due to the community I joined in the metaverse of Upland. I am very grateful for her guidance and willingness to share her vast knowledge and the generosity of including me as part of this project. As I said previously, networking is not my strong suit, and this has definitely opened me up to the importance of making connections and being involved in the community. It feels very weird to say but I really hope you enjoy "our" book.

Table of Contents

The Interviews

SMITH2VR

Father And Son Bond Due to Upland

When did you join Upland and who introduced you?

April 1, 2021, My Son (Zanysocks) got me involved.

How do you serve or are recognized in the community?

I've joined a couple of Discords. I attended the *Light It Upland Vegas 2022 Event*. I brought in a friend of mine and have piqued the interest of others.

Why did you join and what do you think is in Upland's future?

I first joined Upland because I was intrigued by the concept. I continue to play on a daily basis because it holds my interest. One of the first properties I bought was a Marina, I continue to hold this property because I believe that someday we will have boats and people that do not have Ocean front property will need a place to keep their boats. I am patiently waiting for the release of my city so I can race my son to buy my home. If he gets it, he is going to charge me an arm and a leg for it. Excited for the release of other countries especially when we go to England. I lived in Scotland for a while and traveled all over England, and I am looking forward to buying up places I have visited. I play several P2E games and Upland is by far my favorite.

LAKEGIRL

Lives In Upland, That's Upland, Ca

When did you join Upland and who introduced you?

March 2022, I live in Upland, California so when I saw the booth at NFT LA I had to join.

How do you serve or are recognized in the community?

I was the only one at Genesis week who actually lives in Upland. As I am new to Upland, I am still learning. I was so excited to attend Genesis week to learn from others in the community.

Why did you join and what do you think is in Upland's future?

I joined Upland because I believe there will be growth in the metaverse and with each property being an NFT, I see potential. I do not have thousands to put into the game like the chief executives.

I was able to buy my parent's old house in Granada Hill, CA, and I am looking forward to Upland, CA opening one day. I believe as NFT's grow, the property values in the game can truly grow. It's hard to believe people can make additional income from a game like people do in the real estate market but it can happen here.

By: Tammy Revard, AKA LAKEGIRL

HAMTINGS

New Property Owner in Both Universes

When did you join Upland and who introduced you?

July 2021. My friend, as he is known in Upland, UMBRELLABOY introduced me.

How do you serve or are recognized in the community?

I serve the Upland community at the moment by participating in treasure hunts (see glossary). the purchasing of properties, building structures on these parcels and I converse with other players and join meetups when I can to stay informed.

Why did you join and what do you think is in Upland's future?

I am currently a new landowner of 13 acres in real life with no experience owning land whatsoever. I decided to rise to the challenge to develop this raw land, at the same time UPLAND was introduced to me and I got this epiphany that if this game was geared toward land ownership and development of communities, I can combine my real-life experience and add it to the new virtual property ownership and allow both realities to teach me about the other. The future of Upland in my eyes will be the next way for people to own and trade virtual properties in the safety of their space and empower that individual to see the world with a new filter offered by the exposure to Upland.

By: Whitney Ham, AKA HAMTINGS

UMBRELLABOY

Curious And Open to Discover New Ways

When did you join Upland and who introduced you?

March 2021. I discovered Upland during late night web surfing about NFT's and Blockchain games.

How do you serve or are recognized in the community?

I find myself exploring a variety of Upland communities and cheerleading for some amazing and passionate Uplanders. My own 'Big Idea' may be just around the corner.

Why did you join and what do you think is in Upland's future?

Initially I joined out of boredom without any prior knowledge of NFT's, blockchain, or play-to-earn games. I skeptically put in $5, bought my first property in Brooklyn and flipped it for a few more. What is the point of this game? Is it an investment? Where are the rules? Would I someday own the digital version of my home? (Yes!). I soon learned about Discord and discovered a world of characters with funny names – a crazy intersection of crypto investors, gamers, coders, digital artists, and a few scammers. Part wild west, part college dormitory, part never-ending cocktail party filled with people I would never come across IRL(in real life). I found myself meeting some in person, first at a bar in my hometown and then traveling to Vegas. You are seeing people you have met on the Internet, my teenagers ask me. What happened to online safety? I have no good answer. As Upland introduced each new city and game-play mechanic, I can feel this world shifting, much to some players' dismay. But many also speak excitedly of the vast potential of Layer 2 and Web3 (see glossary) concepts I did not understand until a few months ago. I am not certain what the future holds for Upland, but I figure I will stick around awhile and find out.

TEDDYPIG

Helpful Community Member

When did you join Upland and who introduced you?

Feb/March of 2021. I found out about Upland through an advertisement in the Brave browser (it is very crypto friendly). I had just heard about how Virtual Real Estate could be a thing of the future and here was this ad for Virtual Real Estate, so I decided to check it out. How do you serve or are recognized in the community?

How do you serve or are recognized in the community?

I don't think I "serve" anything in the Upland Community directly, but I have been and try to be helpful to any players who need it.

Why did you join and what do you think is in Upland's future?

I have been around for a while now and in the early days I would take part in visit raids. This was where established players in Upland would help new players get to Upland status by visiting their properties multiple times in a row. In a way it was an early money transfer thing, but also fun for both parties. I loved reading the excitement from new players who just had 5 or 6 established players, usually Director and Up, come to their property and load them up with around 30-40 visits. I remember a funny thing about it too, we'd tell them, go to your property, and raise the visit fee to the max. It was confusing to them at first, but they got it after they got the visits. Some new players would get so excited they wanted to instantly turn around and pay it forward, lol (laughing out loud). We had to tell them not too and this led to explaining some of the finer details of the game.

JASMILLS

Founder Of Century Citizens Executives

When did you join Upland and who introduced you?

The beginning(2018/2019?). I had some San Francisco(first city) original Mints. I was introduced by a Crypto YouTuber named XRP CHIZ from one of his videos where he recommended investing in Upland for its tremendous potential.

How do you serve or are recognized in the community?

I am the founder of a node in Upland, called Century Citizens Executives in Century City LA. It became popular. My community has many top players and YouTubers along with many extremely talented members from the Upland Metaverse. Many players are aware of our discord and may have heard about our community in various YouTube Videos from some of the top Youtubers. We also have recently started a YouTube channel and plan on developing it to its maximum potential to help promote Upland.

Why did you join and what do you think is in Upland's future?

I joined Upland originally as an investment. After signing, I quickly grew passionate about the game because of my love of Monopoly and strategy type games. I believe that we are in the early stages of another Gilded Age. This future economic boom will bring with it the most exciting and advanced technologies that the world has ever seen or thought possible. At some point, Upland will hit mainstream adoption and explode. The players and communities that helped to build the foundations for this mass adoption will be greatly rewarded for their efforts. The future is so bright because of the many amazing communities that are popping up with each new city release. The most amazing part about Upland is the people and the amazing memorable interactions and experiences that you have with each other. To me, that will power the future for Upland as those experiences continue to multiply at an ever-increasingly-fast pace.

BEN68

Samurai Aquatics Metaventure Founder

When did you join Upland and who introduced you?

January 13th, 2020. Introduced by The Bad Crypto Podcast. Podcast titled 'Blockchain Gaming Goes Mainstreet with Upland' [January 12, 2020] and a description that included information about a blockchain based monopoly-like game dealing with real-world properties, caught my eye.

How do you serve or are recognized in the community?

I am the creator of the node development concept for coordinated property development. I founded the following: Outdoor Decor Metaventure - Samurai Aquatics 2020; Node development team - Upland Development United 2021; Metatainment platform - Metaverse Ventures Entertainment 2022. I co-host several Metaverse and Upland-related shows on YouTube and Spotify etc. I have been a highly active community member since the very early days on Telegram (before Discord).

Morecheese is my best meta-mate and co-host in everything I do that's Upland related. Without her stepping up her active engagement at some key points in our, at times, very difficult history of Upland Development United, I would have disengaged from involvement in the community long ago.

Why did you join and what do you think is in Upland's future?

I had been playing around with blockchain since 2017, was a hobby game developer, a mobile game beta tester and of course have been a monopoly fan since I was a child. The simple but intuitive and idle-clicker type gameplay at the time hooked me immediately and I've gone in deeper and deeper ever since. As for Upland's future, I defer to that classic line from Terminator: "The future is not set. There is no fate but what we make for ourselves.". I don't know where Upland is headed or even what it's going to look like at the end of 2022, let alone 'in the future'. I do know that no matter what its fate is, I will be a large and actively engaged presence within it

M O R E C H E E S E

C0-Admin of Upland Development United

When did you join Upland and who introduced you?

March 14, 2021, I heard 2 people talking about it in alien worlds (another P2E game) server (in discord).

How do you serve or are recognized in the community?

BEN68 and I both manage the nodes within Upland as well as created spark trains (groups building together) to get the members in the UDU to build faster. We also co admin MVE, our umbrella company where we showcase our YouTube shows "Whine and Cheese in the Metaverses Show", "UDU Podcast", and "Metaventures Adventures". I manage a node in the Bronxdale neighborhood in the Bronx Under the UDU umbrella. I also am a partner with BEN68 and Detech in an Upland Outdoor Decor Metaventure named "Samurai Aquatics". I am a UCN(Upland Contributers Network) member and UCN Broadcaster for Upland.

Why did you join and what do you think is in Upland's future?

During COVID19 I started looking into new things to pass the time. I found Alien Worlds and that took a great 3 months of my time and made me want to investigate more projects, that is where I found Upland. The bad reviews were the first thing I noticed in the Google Play Store. I am not the type of person to go based solely on reviews, so I did my own research and joined Discord, Twitter, and watched some community videos. When I was convinced that the bad reviews were because most people aren't comfortable with a game that has a bit of a steep learning curve, I downloaded Upland and started in Fresno, where I minted my first two props(properties). I invested 10K USD at most and my net worth is now 45 mil UPX (45K USD). I have a lot of faith in Upland. Compared to the other Metaverses: Sandbox, Decentral Land etc., I love the game play in Upland, their roadmap for the future and attended the 2022 Genesis Event in Vegas. Upland is constantly announcing new things and evolving.

By: Angela Marchese, AKA, MORCHEESE

DEATHENDER

3D Designer, Known as Detech on Discord

When did you join Upland and who introduced you?

April 3, 2021. It was advertised in the Brave browser.

How do you serve or are recognized in the community?

I have made gifs for the Upland show and work with the 3D artist community to learn and understand how to make 3D assets for Upland.

Why did you join and what do you think is in Upland's future?

I joined because was something different to what I have seen before. I played the game by myself for months before discovering the Upland Discord. From that moment on was when I really understood what Upland was. To me Upland is the community, and the community is great – it's responsive, and always there to help. There are so many amazing people. Earlier this year I decided to learn 3D modeling and I have been doing it since. If it wasn't for the Upland community, I probably never would. Overall, I love the game and the community, and I hope to see Upland collaborate with other projects to really build a true metaverse.

When joining Upland, most players don't realize that the UI (user interface) is just a façade and then fall down the rabbit hole like I did. I look back with sorrow at my worry-free pre-Upland days when I didn't know what to do with my time. Since I found out what Upland discord was and got to know and collaborate with many creative and amazing people in the community, the game was never the same for me. Starting with Morecheese teaching me how to make my own NFTs and Lilli and many other amazing 3D artists helping me learn Blender, it must be said that Upland community is one of the most open and helpful gaming communities I have ever encountered.

So, to any new/future players reading this book: If you want to learn what a metaverse is, join Upland! Don't forget to visit me in my cell when your over at San Francisco and remember, all good things come with time! lots and lots of time! And don't forget to visit my Upland server and win some of my NFTs.

HACKER

Co-Owner and Developer for UPXLand

When did you join Upland and who introduced you?

August 31, 2020. Found it via the Brave Browser (another browser option like Chrome or Safari) as an ad.

How do you serve or are recognized in the community?

When I started playing Upland I saw that there was no great way of getting data and information about properties. So early 2021 I started coding and building uplandworld.me which was renamed to upx.world.and it became the biggest and only data source from February 2021 to July 2021 when I sold it to another Uplander. I then stopped playing and came back in January 2022. The website I sold was not maintained and eventually got shut down. So as soon as I saw that, I contacted another player called IKris. He had started to build something but was far from finished, so I joined him and started UPX Land which I now am a Co-owner and developer for.

Why did you join and what do you think is in Upland's future?

I think the community was the reason why I stayed. I love developing and creating tools for others, especially when you do it for people that really appreciate you for it. I think Upland is on the right track for the future. My guess is that they want to build a platform which other games and developers can use in the future. The game itself will just be one of many but the infrastructure they are building will be used by more than just Upland, the game. They want to make it easier for normal developers to utilize and build on top of the WEB3 (blockchain) technology.

By: Kevin Kuusela, AKA, HACKER

TOSSHEAD

Co-Winner of Genesis Design Challenge '22

When did you join Upland and who introduced you?

March 202. I saw an ad on Brave browser.

How do you serve or are recognized in the community?

I am maybe best known, but certainly most proud, of being involved in winning the Genesis week vehicle design competition, with my business partner and great friend *Shaktilyn.*

Why did you join and what do you think is in Upland's future?

"Shak" and I both see the tremendous opportunities (creative, social and financial) in web 3 technology and agree that Upland's "real world map" and mobile app make it a lead contender to become a significant hub of the future Metaverse.

The opportunities at this stage seem infinite, but those who focus on the formulas that are adopted in the future will have a hand in shaping history.

JMAC1911

Beloved Son-In-Law

When did you join Upland and who introduced you?

December 20, 2021 - Reddit (internet chat platform-think Facebook)

How do you serve or are recognized in the community?

I hold property as an investment and invited Shaktilyn, my mother-in-law to join Upland in JAN 2022.

Why did you join and what do you think is in Upland's future?

I joined Upland because I was tired of always being late to the party (I missed out on Bitcoin). When I heard about virtual land in the metaverse, I started looking into it and was disappointed to see that plots of land were already selling for thousands of dollars. And then I heard about Upland and discovered property in Upland was still very affordable. So, I bought a bunch of properties, and I am holding them as an investment. I believe the Metaverse is still in its infancy, and that it will eventually become a mainstream and normal part of our lives. I think Upland is the most promising of all the metaverses because it is mapped to the real world and will naturally attract businesses and customers at the most basic and intuitive level.

SHAKTILYN

Co-Winner of Genesis Design Challenge '22

When did you join Upland and who introduced you?

January 3, 2022, introduced by my son-in-law, SniperFrank#0116, IGN JMAC1911. He said that we were "late to the party" with Bitcoin, but this was our chance to be among the early adopters of virtual land ownership. I thank him for expanding my world!

How do you serve or are recognized in the community?

I am well known for helping to bring the first Artisan vehicle, "The Imagination Van" into the Upland metaverse, together with my great friend and business partner, TossHed.

During my time in Vegas for Genesis Week 2022, I was struck by what a beautiful community we have here in Upland. The experience instilled in me a sense of oneness, and the desire to support each other's projects. I believe tribalism is destructive; whereas collaboration, mutual support, and good will, can help us build a better metaverse for all.

It is my great honor to be working with UPX World: a web3, layer-2 gaming platform launching on Steam and coming soon to the Upland metaverse. I am one of the founders and leaders of Creedmoor Hub; TossHed's partner on the Avenue of Fashion as well as The Toss-Shak design team; a leader of IDA Monero; and a member of multiple projects:

To prove the power of cross-community collaboration, we recently conducted an experiment to see what 24 players from 5 different groups could achieve together.

We believe we have proven that working together brings tremendous good to the Upland community, the metaverse, and also to the real world.

Why did you join and what do you think is in Upland's future?

I discovered cryptocurrencies in October 2021. Topics like "the metaverse" and "virtual land ownership" both baffled and intrigued me. When I entered the Upland metaverse, I fumbled around with my Block Explorer, and impulsively bought my first property. It was the beginning of a most remarkable journey! Shortly thereafter, I realized Upland was about more than virtual real estate. It was actually about people; about building something bigger together than anyone could ever build alone. I've been privileged to meet the most amazing individuals with huge hearts, dreams, integrity, and talents! Each is a gift to me! I'm honored to call them my friends, and excited for the future. We are in the dawn of a new era — the metaverse (web3) era — where people from all corners of the world live, play, and work together in the same space. Physical boundaries no longer dictate who we meet, or with whom we associate. In fact, the only divisions in the metaverse are those we choose to create ourselves. Why not build this new world to reflect the best of humanity? If we choose to use the metaverse for good, it can offer great opportunities for global peace and cross-cultural understanding. My short journey into this realm has already blown my mind, but we are still in the wee hours of morning. Our ultimate destination is a story that is ours to write.

DESJAAK

Amazed By the Upland Community

When did you join Upland and who introduced you?

Summer of 2021. I think it was Womplay that had me registering, but it was Brave Browser that kept reminding me that Upland was a thing. CAFE MORGADOR was the one teaching me all the ropes around this place.

How do you serve or are recognized in the community?

I think I'm known for research, design, or both. For research I have been a part of Analytic Assassins, where we do city release research for new cities that come out in Upland. All this information is shared freely with the players of Upland, to level the playing field for everyone. Besides that, I create designs for Upland. From metaventure artwork to in-game assets, this is the part of Upland that I like most. You can already find my design in Upland: the Assassins Courtyard building in Chicago, and the Genesis Week Meta Space Invader ornament (BASICALLY A COVER FOR YOUR BUILDING) – with many more to come.

Why did you join and what do you think is in Upland's future?

I joined Upland because the world was in lockdown - I stayed because of the community. I have never been a part of a digital community before, I wasn't even on Discord before I joined Upland (it took me a week to find it). I've gotten to know amazing people, who are creating even more amazing projects. The players in Upland are the actual value, they bring so much. From spark exchanges to nodes, new players help and now layer 2 experiences (see glossary), this community keeps amazing me and here is where I see the future for Upland. I hope to be part of that, with the Assassins Park node (Avalon Park, Chicago), new layer 2 experiences, and hopefully most of all: more UGC(user generated content) designs in game. See you in the future at my Upland blueprint store!

K C B C

Known On Discord as Uplando

When did you join Upland and who introduced you?

November 25th, 2020. DappRadar (Website that lists Decentralized applications-which Upland is)

How do you serve or are recognized in the community?

On Discord, I am known as Uplando. I serve by being an active Discord community member. Co-Founding *The Upland Cafe Voice Channel*, Broadcasting a radio style program that features guests and show regulars that discuss news and information about Upland, the earth's Metaverse mapped to the real world. The show is recorded live daily Monday to Friday at 7PM PT on Uplands official discord server in *The Upland Café Voice Channel*. I operate a Block Explorers shop. I was one of the first 20 players to be approved for a metaventure NFT shop in upland.

Why did you join and what do you think is in Upland's future?

I joined Upland as a result of having a bullish(positive) outlook on NFTs. Once I found Uplands Discord server it reinforced my belief that the project was going to have a successful run.

CMAVS

Upland Master Builder

When did you join Upland and who introduced you?

November 2021. I saw Dirk (one of the founders) in an interview online while I was researching Metaverse related content.

How do you serve or are recognized in the community?

I am an Upland Master Builder. I have 3 structure models that won community build contests (Mavs Perch Manhattan, Cornerstone Rutherford and KCAD Kansas City). I have one Decor ornament in game; Lakhes Rocket Llama that I designed, modeled, and won for the Genesis 2022 community contest. I'm the creator and founder of the DRL, Detroit Rally League, a racing community in Detroit. Victory Motors & Victory Motorsports, a vehicle design and manufacturing endeavor focused on cars, trucks and motorsports racing. I'm also the founder of several race zone nodes including the MCAAD: motor city automotive arts district and CARZ node in Arlington Texas.

Why did you join and what do you think is in Upland's future?

I joined Upland to be a metaverse entrepreneur. To utilize my creative design and 3D modeling skills to develop digital art and design companies to design, build, manufacture and sell an array of 3D building structures, decor, and vehicles models in the Upland Metaverse.

THANKMELATER
Co-Host Of the UPX Podcast

When did you join Upland and who introduced you?

January 2022. I found Upland through an ad on Twitter.

How do you serve or are recognized in the community?

I'm cohost of the longest running Upland themed broadcast - The UPX Podcast. I helped start and run some of the most recognizable brands in the Upland community including UPX.World and Upland.Wiki. I'm also the owner of the Genesis property :)

Why did you join and what do you think is in Upland's future?

I joined Upland because as an Enterprise Architect a lot of my clients were wanting to get into blockchain for supply chain management. I saw an ad on Twitter for a new Monopoly like blockchain game -Upland (and it had a fun Llama). Outside of work I'm an avid gamer! So, this was a great chance for me to try out this new tech in a format I enjoyed. I think Upland's underlying technology, mobile focus, and brilliant leadership team put Upland well ahead of the current generation of Metaverses.

By: Joe Westrich, AKA THANKMELATER

HUMBLELIFE

Houseless Advocate

When did you join Upland and who introduced you?

Summer of 2022. Technically I introduced myself to Upland surfing Google play.

How do you serve or are recognized in the community?

I try to serve Upland by influencing node interaction and collaboration, especially those involved with charitable and social causes, I'm usually recognized as being involved heavily with social causes around homelessness, and Social Cause Gamification, or P2D (Play to Donate).

Why did you join and what do you think is in Upland's future?

I joined Upland in an effort to find a way to help local homeless individuals and families, I can't do outreach as much due to some physical and psychological issues, but still wanted a way to give back. Originally this started as an investment idea, but as I've learned more, there's much more potential than I originally thought. So, I've invested my own lil change into Layer 1&2 in hopes of getting my account to be a full-time business and gain respectable partnerships with communities like Wood-Hood, Badican House, URL, DRL, UPX World, Creedmoor, Copacabana.... so many I can't list!

UPX World and its connection with Upland have created an atmosphere of welcoming new people into spaces they may not have ever gotten the opportunity to otherwise. I'm glad to be a part of seeing all this come together and the possibilities for changing issues like homelessness, hunger, and more in the real world is the best thing that could ever come from a Metaverse.

BLUERAIN

Posts Cheapest Properties Prices

When did you join Upland and who introduced you?

January 2022, and was introduced through YouTube.

How do you serve or are recognized in the community?

I post daily content on the cheapest property prices in all Upland cities on YouTube and TikTok, and I am a member of the Upland Contributor Network of broadcasters(UCN)

Why did you join and what do you think is in Upland's future?

After years of playing the mobile game *War and Order* and dumping money into it monthly to buy gems to protect my castle, I was immediately drawn into Upland by the potential of a game that I could not only play but earn money from playing the game. The concept of playing to earn was the thing that grabbed me; the connection to Monopoly was the hook. The concept of earning money while playing a virtual property game that was akin to one of the World's most classic board games was exciting to me. Playing the game has been and has remained exciting since my beginning days in Upland. With Upland being in a plethora of news sources (crypto, gaming, and business) and with Upland being compared to other metaverses like Sandbox and Decentraland, I see a big future for Upland ahead. The player base is growing by the day, and more importantly, Upland is growing in its visions and following through with its promises. Players remain committed because they see Upland as a stable project with immense potential. As more people become aware of the metaverse, the value of the current NFTs held by Upland players is likely to multiply exponentially.

ZWYVREN

A Metacorp Executive

When did you join Upland and who introduced you?

September 2021. Introduced by Google Ads and the Upland Show.

How do you serve or are recognized in the community?

I'm a MetaCorp executive for Upland Meta Corp (parent company for Upland Construction Company (UCC) and UMC Financial (merger of Bank of Upland and MetaFran Holdings), I'm also the founder of Upland Racing League and co-founder of Citadel FC (a World of Futbol team.)

Why did you join and what do you think is in Upland's future?

I was looking for games where I had ownership of my assets. Too many mobile games are just money traps and I wanted something I could resell (like Magic the Gathering cards.) I think Upland is one of the first P2E games that is getting it right - they are establishing themselves as a layer 1 platform where the community/players will be able to create content and be more entrepreneurial. The idea of a MetaCorp (Metaverse Corporation) executive with some financial benefit is a true possibility in Upland and that is what I see as the biggest impact of Upland (and games that follow this pattern)

MUCIDA

Owner Of Upland Brasil YouTube Channel

When did you join Upland and who introduced you?

April 2021, introduced through Brave Browser.

How do you serve or are recognized in the community?

I am the owner of Upland Brasil YouTube channel and Instagram profile. We have more than 5k subscribers, more than 100 videos with tips and tutorials about Upland, we put on live shows every week to talk with the players. I am also a UCN official member as a broadcaster and moderator in Discord. I was also voted as the player of the year in 2022 =)

Why did you join and what do you think is in Upland's future?

I joined Upland because it was easy to see that buying and selling properties as NFTs that are also mapped in the real world would be something huge. I saw (and keep seeing) a lot of good opportunities there. It is stable, strong, diversified, and also Upland is the easiest way to get access to the NFT world. NFT's and metaverse are just starting, we are early adopters, and this game is writing something great in the history of this new era of Web 3.0 (see glossary).

RADISHHEAD

YouTuber Of Upland Analysis

When did you join Upland and who introduced you?

April 2021 from a Reddit advertisement. It's very rare I click an ad, but I'd been hearing a lot about the metaverse and wanted to see what Upland was all about (plus, Miles the Llama was a very appealing character — great design!).

How do you serve or are recognized in the community?

I run the YouTube channel Upland Analysis. I try to act as a middle ground between some of the real 'beginner'-level channels and guides, and the more expert-level advice you can find on Discord. I target the Uplanders who are fairly active but may not have the time to log onto Discord every single day, or to truly consider the implications of the major economic updates.

Also, my collection predictions are probably my most popular videos — people appreciate having a familiar face talk them through the key neighbourhoods and streets of a new city!

Why did you join and what do you think is in Upland's future?

I joined Upland on a whim! Unlike a lot of the 'OGs', who seem to have been engrossed in Metaverse and Crypto culture for years, I was far removed from that world. I enjoy video games and board games and found appeal in Upland from that perspective. But over time I've gained more acknowledgement of the value of NFTs in gaming, and the role that Upland plays in that journey.

I'm known as a very positive voice when it comes to the future of Upland, and people often ask me why. For me, I feel like I truly understand the scope of what the co-founders are trying to achieve here, and if it works, I (and many others) are going to make a lot of money! But ultimately, it's a risky play and I completely understand the less bullish side of the argument. Upland is aiming to become a significant part of a wider multi-platform metaverse, alongside Animoca... only time will tell if they arise as a leading player.

LOYLDOYL

Voted 2022 Broadcaster of the Year

When did you join Upland and who introduced you?

November of 2020. Many people don't know this, but I was friends with X1theGamer before he became community manager for Upland. We shared an office where we would make YouTube content together and I remember we both downloaded Upland on our phones the same day as his interview.

How do you serve or are recognized in the community?

I was recognized as "2022 Broadcaster of the Year" at the first in person Genesis Week Las Vegas in June of 2022. I received this award for my YouTube podcast and how-to videos that I make about Upland. It's been super rewarding to be able to create content that has allowed other people to be able to find success.

Why did you join and what do you think is in Upland's future?

I am a gamer and an entrepreneur and when I saw the opportunity to mix a strategy game with a money-making opportunity, I was hooked. I've always been intrigued by the idea of the metaverse as depicted in the movie, *Ready Player One*. I think writing is on the wall that we're immersed in our digital lives and the metaverse is going to be a success no matter what.

I believe Dirk and Idan and the leaders of Upland have a very keen understanding of economics, which is a vital key to success for any metaverse. I also believe that being a digital version of our actual world is another key to success for Upland. The metaverse is a digital representation of what we want to have in the physical world so being able to have our digital lives as a cooler and more exciting mirror to our actual life will be a major success as the metaverse gets more advanced. I'm most excited for avatars to come in the future and at that point I think digital fashion will be massive to the Upland economy. It will also present an opportunity for us to create a more sustainable future for our planet with less waste as we can acquire more digital fashion than physical fashion.

LILAPPLE

Active Participant in The Crypto-Space

When did you join Upland and who introduced you?

I discovered Upland while researching play-to-earn gaming options. As an active participant in the crypto-space since 2017, NFT and play-to-earn projects were of kindred interest to my cryptocurrency research. My initial inquiries into the NFT real-estate were met with discouragement due to the high cost of entry. When I discovered Upland, the ease of mobile gameplay accessibility and free-to-play elements were too enticing to not give it a try!

How do you serve or are recognized in the community?

Within Upland, I am a community builder, advisor, and liaison to the metaverse for new players. My primary pursuits include time in service to community building through participation on the Century City Node Network Leadership Team and advisory and consultation efforts toward developing engaging level II utility projects such as the Floating Farms initiative.

Why did you join and what do you think is in Upland's future?

I joined in a state of curiosity with the intention of exploring the Upland Metaverse and generating a bit of petty cash. Mobile app accessibility and nominal financial threshold for entry made the opportunity to good to pass-up. I have STAYED for the community building, infinite and evolving layer two interface possibilities, and profit potential that has vastly outpaced my wildest expectations. Furthermore, myriad touchpoints in the layer 1 interface will allow for more immersive experiences including casual and competitive gamification, galleries, NFT communities, and fee-for-service enterprises. The final key element to Upland's ultimate success are collaborative efforts between the Upland team, commercial partners, and the player community. There is a vast and largely untapped pool of talent residing within the player base of Upland. It is within the minds of the players themselves that the future of Upland resides.

By: Curtis Mick, AKA LILAPPLE

HUMANSIM

Hid Being a Minor from Upland

When did you join Upland and who introduced you?

On the 30th of April in 2021 through an advertisement I got through the App Store on my phone.

How do you serve or are recognized in the community?

I was definitely not the type of demographic Upland was likely looking for; I was a very casual 16-year-old gamer in high school looking for a good time, not really looking to get money out of the game. Being a youthful member of the community was definitely difficult, as the Terms of Service refused service to minors, leaving me to hide my true age from many. Even so, whenever I disclosed my age to someone I trusted, I ran the risk of that person attempting to blackmail me or take advantage of me. However, being under twenty in a sea of older folks allowed me to get the mentoring I needed to help me navigate Upland in a manner that wouldn't jeopardize my Upland portfolio or my interactions with others.

The first project I really took up was the Upland Transit Guide, which was a series of art pieces I made displaying all navigation routes around Upland. Though Upland has grown beyond my means to continue that map, I now create the Upland Minting Guides for upcoming cities, allowing players who have pertinent duties outside of Upland to have adequate research for collection speculation in future cities.

Why did you join and what do you think is in Upland's future?

In terms of Upland's future, I'll be honest and say that I'm uncertain due to the general chaos of our world. Blockchain can be a flourishing medium for communication and gaming, acting, in my eyes at least, almost like the grand mall in every town that everyone flocks to. However, just like many malls in the United States, they can become ghost towns when interest fades, becoming a cascade of closure after closure. No matter the way Upland goes, I'll be enjoying the ride with all of its bumps along the way.

TDAVIS

Helped Onboard Many into Upland

When did you join Upland and who introduced you?

August 2020, I discovered it via banner ad from stateofthedapps.com.

How do you serve or are recognized in the community?

I feel like this question could be better answered by any of the dozens (if not hundreds) of players that started in 2021 who I helped guide their onboarding into Upland and in many cases, NFTs. Some of the quantifiable highlights include laid the foundation for what would eventually become the Upland Moderators. Helped hundreds obtain Uplander status and go on to be successful players.

Held the #1 rank in Discord activity for 1+ years, and currently still Top 10 overall.

Charitably distributed $10k USD+ value in properties and UPX to new players, so that they might prosper early-on

One of a very, very few number (maybe less than 5?) of Hero Badge holders; helped expose a major exploit ("mint any property, locked or unlocked, from any location", bug) that would have resulted in irreparable game damage, if not destroyed it completely.

Publish0x Contest Winner (Feb '21) for community themed content "UplandLI: An Origin Story" article, which was influential to how "Upland Nodes" operate today.

Why did you join and what do you think is in Upland's future?

I joined from the perspective of an aspiring dApp developer. In the subsequent 2+ years, I've watched as Upland has positioned itself as a leader in web3 tokenomics (a testament to their founders) and created a platform that will allow individuals to easily onboard into the Metaverse. I, forsee their 3rd Party Development network taking Upland to the next level and really pushing the boundaries of what a Metaverse dApp should be.

KIDKONNRY

Upland News Reporter, Owns Analytic Assassins

When did you join Upland and who introduced you?

March of 2021. A Brave Browser Advertisement got me interested. I started learning about the game on YouTube.

How do you serve or are recognized in the community?

I served as an Upland Discord Moderator for over a Year. My Name in Discord is CaFe MogadoR I helped solve many disputes between players and am known for my light touch moderating. I also helped start up Analytic Assassins (A research server) and am now the owner of it. I have Desjaak run things there for me. More recently, I have moved the news section and voice chat from the Analytic Assassins to a new server called Upland Daily. Upland Daily is the community's first dedicated news server to Upland. We cover daily happenings in the game in short headlines with occasional context added to explain deeper topics.

Why did you join and what do you think is in Upland's future?

I joined Upland because I have always loved Monopoly and City Builder type of Games. I am also interested and trained in finance and stocks and learned crypto when it started picking up steam. Upland scratched quite a few itches as far as features it offered. Then I went onto discord and discovered a very active and passionate community. About 3 months after joining X1 asked if I would be a Discord Moderator and about the same time, I helped create the Assassins. I think Upland has a bright future. We are in turbulent times and most markets are being tested. Upland has fair rather well compared to other markets and projects. There are quirks and fowl ups here and there, but the game is progressing. I feel the next bull market in crypto will drive a lot of money to Upland when people take and park some profits. I myself am focusing on the Avalon Park node in Chicago. It's the official node of Analytic Assassins and we are very excited to get it going. I am also focusing on continuing to develop Analytic Assassins, especially the Chat and Voice room side of the server.

CRYOGENIKZ

Built Treasure Hunting Map for Highest Profitability

When did you join Upland and who introduced you?

September of 2021.

How do you serve or are recognized in the community?

I often participate in a Facebook group on Upland, answer questions people have about the game.

Why did you join and what do you think is in Upland's future?

My business partner and I got into it for the passive income. The monthly revenue is what keeps me coming back for more properties. I like to buy and flip my properties to buy something that earns more rent than what I sold. I have built a treasure hunting map to allow me to treasure hunt while keeping send fees down to a minimal amount to ensure the highest profitability. We needed a place to invest our money and Upland seems to be a great candidate with a bright future.

SATOSHI

Metaventure Owner, Dao Creator

When did you join Upland and who introduced you?

September 2020. Who introduced me is an interesting story as I had no clue what a metaverse was the day that I found Upland. I was initially looking for a Tron Defi application when I stumbled upon Dapp Radar. When looking at the top 10 list, I saw Upland at number 8. I was intrigued by the idea of digital real estate and the competitive nature of Monopoly, so I thought I'd give it a try. One month later, I was hooked.

How do you serve or are recognized in the community?

Initially, I had started with the UCN Network to promote Upland and eventually climbed to the Moderator role prior to launching my own Dapps on WAXP & ETH. When interacting with the Upland Community, I always put myself in the other person's shoes by providing my expertise to educate on how to approach a potential business dealing or opportunity within the game. I think my best-known traits in the Metaverse are being a trustworthy person that will always look out for an Uplander's best interest & the Uplander that has a competitive obsession with having the best dividend yield ratio in the game. Community is everything and I wouldn't be where I am today without the Upland Community!

By:Steven Tucker Merkler AKA SATOSHISVIEW

Tidbits & Journal Prompts

Note: If you have the NFT version, or do not like to write in a book, and want to receive a download of this and all the other journal prompts please send an email to ouruplandbook.com Subject Our Upland Journal Prompts, and we will be happy to send them to you.

TIDBIT

Uplandme, Inc. is a globally distributed organization. Its headquarter is in Silicon Valley where it was founded by Dirk Lueth, Idan Zuckerman, and Mani Honigstein.

Journal Prompt:

If you met the three founders of Upland Inc, and could ask each one question, what would it be? Why this question? ?

_____

_____

_____

_____

_____

_____

_____

_____

_____

_____

_____

_____

_____

_____

TIDBIT

Upland is a digital real estate game with virtual properties mapped to the real world. Upland uses block-chain technology enabling anyone to buy, sell and trade NFT (Non-Fungible Tokens) real estate for a profit.

Journal Prompt:

What property would you love to buy? Who would you need to race to get there first?

_____

_____

_____

_____

_____

_____

_____

_____

_____

_____

_____

_____

_____

_____

TIDBIT

San Francisco was the original city released in the game. There is now many more American cities that have been released and properties and partnerships expanded beyond the United States into South America and Europe.

Journal Prompt:

What city do you think would be a great edition to the Upland metaverse? Why?

_____

_____

_____

_____

_____

_____

_____

_____

_____

_____

_____

_____

_____

TIDBIT

Nodes are communities of players within the game in certain neighborhoods. Ben68, a player in the game created the word node when he started Midtown Terrace, San Francisco, the original and therefore genesis node.

Journal Prompt:

Do you know how to join a node? Which neighborhood do you want to join a node in? Explain?

_____

_____

_____

_____

_____

_____

_____

_____

_____

_____

_____

_____

_____

_____

TIDBIT

Since San Francisco, there are now many more American cities that have been released and properties and partnerships expanded beyond the United States into South America and Europe.

Journal Prompt:

What city do you think would be a great edition to the Upland metaverse? Why?

_____

_____

_____

_____

_____

_____

_____

_____

_____

_____

_____

_____

_____

_____

_____

_____

TIDBIT

When Upland opened up Rio de Janeiro Brazil, property sold out very quickly. It was the first city to be released outside of the continental United States.

Journal Prompt:

Have you been to Brazil in real life or in the Upland Metaverse? Where did you go? Is there any property you have your eye on and want to buy?

_____

_____

_____

_____

_____

_____

_____

_____

_____

_____

_____

_____

_____

_____

TIDBIT

Upland is an NFT project which means it is recorded immutably (it cannot be changed), on the blockchain. All NFT's are stored and recorded this way which is what gives value to these digital items. One benefit is that this could eliminate devastating, financial trickery that we read about in the news.

Journal Prompt:

Experts think that almost all-important documents and items will ultimately be recorded in NFT form. From the deed to your home to the receipts you receive when buying your groceries. Do you think this is a good thing?

_____

_____

_____

_____

_____

_____

_____

_____

_____

_____

_____

_____

_____

_____

TIDBIT

Scammers and cheaters are not welcomed in real life nor in Upland and if anyone is found doing something against the rules which are laid out in TOS (Terms of Service) , they are sent to Alcatraz (Upland jail). As in the real world, sometimes we feel people are wrongly accused and other times we are thrilled they are getting the punishment they deserve.

Journal Prompt:

What do you want to do in Upland? How long do you think it will take you? Which friends of yours do you think would like to do this with you? Have you invited them to join Upland?

_____

_____

_____

_____

_____

_____

_____

_____

_____

_____

_____

_____

_____

_____

TIDBIT

TOS stands for Terms of Service which most of us NEVER actually read fully and just click on the "agree" button. It's very important to read the TOC. Should you find out you violated the agreement, it is best to own up to it and resolve the issue as quickly as possible and get back to being in integrity. It will also help you sleep better at night.

Journal Prompt:

Do you always read the Terms of Service when you download an app, game, program? If you realize that you are not following them after the fact, what would you do to remedy the situation?

_____

_____

_____

_____

_____

_____

_____

_____

_____

_____

_____

_____

_____

_____

TIDBIT

The entrepreneurial spirit is obviously alive and well in the Upland metaverse. The options seem open and limitless.

Journal Prompt:

Do you desire to co-own property or a game app with someone? What can you imagine and develop? Who would you work with on this?

_____

_____

_____

_____

_____

_____

_____

_____

_____

_____

_____

_____

_____

_____

_____

_____

TIDBIT

Anywhere there is a digital environment where people congregate, it is a Metaverse. The word Metaverse is still being defined. There are many upcoming Metaverses which are being developed currently, and books on the Metaverse are available to learn more.

Journal Prompt:

Which metaverse are you currently participating in? Do you think they will become one large connected metaverse or will they remain separate entities? What would you like to see happen?

_____

_____

_____

_____

_____

_____

_____

_____

_____

_____

_____

_____

_____

_____

TIDBIT

Players can create a niche audience and outlet for themselves by coming up with individual, partnerships, or group projects that relate to Upland on any platform. For example, a server on Discord, Reddit, a YouTube Channel, a Layer 2 game, designs, and more to sell in Metaverse stores.

Journal Prompt:

What niche could you fit into or create within the community? Is there something that someone is already doing that you could do better or differently?

_____

_____

_____

_____

_____

_____

_____

_____

_____

_____

_____

_____

_____

_____

_____

_____

TIDBIT

Players can create projects connected to Upland. Projects may or may not pay off financially. Working on projects is a great way to make friends and connections along the way that may last a lifetime.

Journal Prompt:

Do you think this effort will pay off in the future? Is it paying off now? Is it more about the journey or more about the results?

_____

_____

_____

_____

_____

_____

_____

_____

_____

_____

_____

_____

_____

_____

_____

TIDBIT

Two Upland players TossHed and Shaktilyn collaborated on creating the first artisan vehicle to enter the Upland metaverse. Their "The Imagination Van," took first place in the Upland Genesis Design Challenge 2022, leading to the formation of a partnership, the Toss-Shak Design Studio. It's great when people get together on a project within the metaverse or in real life and find success.

Journal Prompt:

Who in your real or "digital" life would make a good person to collaborate with? What would you create together?

_____

_____

_____

_____

_____

_____

_____

_____

_____

_____

_____

_____

_____

_____

TIDBIT

UPXland.me allows players to search for many types of information (sale prices, ownerships, transactions, etc.) in the blockchain data. People can create their own games, databases, and environments on top of Upland.

Journal Prompt:

Have you visited UPXland.me? What are your thoughts? Upland wants to make it easier for smaller developers to utilize and build on top of the (blockchain) technology. Is that something that interests you? Explain.

_____

_____

_____

_____

_____

_____

_____

_____

_____

_____

_____

_____

_____

_____

TIDBIT

Upland allows players to use their platform for 3rd party developers to create games or other applications "on top" of Upland's property game. This leaves room for endless possibilities for fun and revenue potential for players.

Journal Prompt:

If you were able to create something "on top" of Upland, what can you imagine creating? Would you create something for fun or revenue or both?

_____

_____

_____

_____

_____

_____

_____

_____

_____

_____

_____

_____

_____

_____

_____

_____

TIDBIT

Layer 2 refers to applications or games built on top of Upland which is a Layer 1 game/app.

Journal Prompt:

What type of layer 2 game would you like to see or create on top of the Upland Metaverse?

_____

_____

_____

_____

_____

_____

_____

_____

_____

_____

_____

_____

_____

_____

TIDBIT

UPX World is a layer 2 game. When you go to Upland you see neighborhoods and properties. When you go to UPX World, it utilizes Upland as a base and a whole other game is overlayed on top of it.

Journal Prompt:

What type of layer 2 game would you like to see or create on top of the Upland Metaverse?

_____

_____

_____

_____

_____

_____

_____

_____

_____

_____

_____

_____

_____

_____

_____

TIDBIT

Upland accepts 3D designs created by players within the game. Some designs have been outsourced so you don't necessarily need to master 3D design programs to contribute.

Journal Prompt:

Are you interested in learning 3D design? Do you have other skills that could be useful in the Upland Universe, such as sales, marketing, etc.? Are you comfortable going on Discord and chatting with people who have the skills you want to learn to see if they can mentor you?

_____

_____

_____

_____

_____

_____

_____

_____

_____

_____

_____

_____

_____

TIDBIT

If you have the skills or connections to design top-notch 3D models, you could make money through it in Upland.

Journal Prompt:

How do you hope Upland collaborates with other projects to really build a true metaverse?

_____

_____

_____

_____

_____

_____

_____

_____

_____

_____

_____

_____

_____

_____

_____

_____

_____

_____

TIDBIT

The members of Upland are known for their charitable giving.

Journal Prompt:

Does it impact you in any way to know that many members of a community support charities? Which one do you support? Which groups would you love to support more?

_____

_____

_____

_____

_____

_____

_____

_____

_____

_____

_____

_____

_____

_____

_____

_____

TIDBIT

Play to Earn or blockchain games are a new thing which drastically change the template of games wherein the players actually have ownership of the items they own in the game and can buy/sell/trade them for a profit or loss.

Journal Prompt:

How familiar are you with Play-to-Earn or blockchain games? What was your initial opinion of having the ability to have ownership of items in a game? Has that opinion changed? How?

_____

_____

_____

_____

_____

_____

_____

_____

_____

_____

_____

_____

_____

_____

TIDBIT

Upland players are known for sharing their knowledge with players, and often help new players get started. A few of the players even started Upland related groups, blogs, and podcasts on YouTube and Discord.

Journal Prompt:

How do find out or keep up with the market trends and where to buy in Upland?

_____

_____

_____

_____

_____

_____

_____

_____

_____

_____

_____

_____

_____

_____

_____

_____

_____

TIDBIT

Upland Analysis is a YouTube Channel started by Radishhead in October 22. It started off giving detailed information on market trends in Upland and where to buy. The channel has diversified more into Upland news. Its ultimate goal and where it remains strong is in being a useful community resource.

Journal Prompt:

How do find out or keep up with the market trends and where to buy in Upland?

_____

_____

_____

_____

_____

_____

_____

_____

_____

_____

_____

_____

_____

_____

TIDBIT

The Upland Show is a podcast dedicated to introducing the Universe to the Metaverse. In the original episodes co-hosts, LOYLODYL and McSqueeb dive into the virtual world of Upland bringing you news, and strategies.

Journal Prompt:

Do you do anything daily to enhance your knowledge, your finances, or your fun? In what ways? Would you listen to a daily podcast about Upland? What would your reasons be?

_____

_____

_____

_____

_____

_____

_____

_____

_____

_____

_____

_____

_____

TIDBIT

Whine and Cheese in the Metaverse is one of several YouTube Shows related to Upland They are one of many content creators on YouTube and other platforms. See *Classifieds* for their links, as week as of others.

Journal Prompt:

What Upland related podcasts have you listened to? What Upland related topics would you like the hosts of *Whine and Cheese in the Metaverse* to talk about? If you were to create content about Upland, what topics would you cover?

_____

_____

_____

_____

_____

_____

_____

_____

_____

_____

_____

_____

_____

_____

_____

_____

TIDBIT

When people join Upland, they need to create a username. What people may not realize is that you cannot change it. It is permanent. This has caused some players to say, "I can't believe I did that." as what they thought would be temporary becomes their handle, or the name people connect or know them by forever.

c

Journal Prompt:

What are your nicknames in games or in real life? Does your nickname fit you? Who gave it to you? If you could choose any name to be known as, what would you choose and why?

_____

_____

_____

_____

_____

_____

_____

_____

_____

_____

_____

TIDBIT

To join Upland, it pays to use a referral link, as you get extra UPX bonus upon your first purchase, the currency used to play the game. You can use this link here. Hi! Check out Upland, a virtual property trading game. If you use this link, Upland will award you with a bonus for your first purchase https://r.upland.me/CHLy.

Journal Prompt:

Reflect on your decision to join Upland using a referral link. How did this initial bonus impact your early experiences in the game?

_____

_____

_____

_____

_____

_____

_____

_____

_____

_____

_____

_____

_____

TIDBIT

When you first join you are a visitor. This requires you to renew a Visa, every 7 days, or any assets you acquired go back into the pool, until you reach 10,000 UPX and become an Uplander.

Journal Prompt:

What strategies did you (will you) use to accumulate 10,000 UPX and transition to the Uplander status?

_____

_____

_____

_____

_____

_____

_____

_____

_____

_____

_____

_____

_____

_____

TIDBIT

When you first join you are a visitor. This requires you to renew a Visa, every 7 days, or any assets you acquired go back into the pool, until you reach 10,000 UPX and become an Uplander.

Journal Prompt:

What strategies did you (will you) use to accumulate 10,000 UPX and transition to the Uplander status?

_____

_____

_____

_____

_____

_____

_____

_____

_____

_____

_____

_____

_____

_____

TIDBIT

KYC means know your customer. It is a way you verify your identity, and it helps to prevent bad actors from taking advantage of players and the game. It is optional. You click on settings in your profile. KYC is also helpful as it needed for getting a daily login bonus, to get Spark. and to get involved in other activities.

Journal Prompt:

What were (are) your reasons for choosing to complete the KYC verification?

_____

_____

_____

_____

_____

_____

_____

_____

_____

_____

_____

_____

TIDBIT

If you are thinking of cashing out of the game, you need a KYC, you also must own property of a minimum of 30 days (for Uplanders) before selling in USD. The number of days decreases the higher your status.

Journal Prompt:

Imagine a scenario of cashing out that would make you smile. What are you thinking?

_____

_____

_____

_____

_____

_____

_____

_____

_____

_____

_____

_____

_____

TIDBIT

If you are thinking of cashing out of the game, you need a KYC, you also must own property of a minimum of 30 days (for Uplanders) before selling in USD. The number of days decreases the higher your status.

Journal Prompt:

Imagine a scenario of cashing out that would make you smile. What are you thinking?

_____

_____

_____

_____

_____

_____

_____

_____

_____

_____

_____

_____

TIDBIT

Anything else you need to learn you can obtain by listening to podcasts, reading blogs, reading the glossary, joining the Upland Discord, and chatting with people in the game and joining the community.

Journal Prompt:

Reflect on the importance of community engagement in shaping your Upland journey and decision-making processes. Who were some of the first people you met in the community that helped you alone?

_____

_____

_____

_____

_____

_____

_____

_____

_____

_____

_____

_____

_____

TIDBIT

Treasuring hunting is a mini game within Upland where you search for a "treasure" by traveling around Upland looking at directional arrow clues trying to locate a treasure chest or Pinata which gives the finder UPX or Spark prizes.

Journal Prompt:

Are you excited by treasure hunting? Have you done it yet?

_____

_____

_____

_____

_____

_____

_____

_____

_____

_____

_____

_____

TIDBIT

To take advantage of an Upland Treasure Hunt you may need to travel to a different city from where you are located. The ways to travel include train, bus, and plane. When you want to go from one location to another within a city, you need to click on the property you want to go to and click send on the property card. When you do so, it costs you a very minimal fee, called the send fee (which goes to the owner of the property). The trick is that you are only allowed so many sends. One way to get more sends is to find a paper airplane in the city you are in.

Journal Prompt:

Would you invest in a treasure hunting map if it led to better results?

_____

_____

_____

_____

_____

_____

_____

_____

_____

_____

_____

TIDBIT

You are important. When you disappear, people in the Community notice. They wonder if you are okay. Release their concerns. Let them know if you are going to take an extended vacation or be away for work.

Journal Prompt:

Do you think of the members of the community you belong(virtual or real life) to as part of your extended family? Explain. Many people have found unexpected new friends and relationships because of Upland, are you excited to discover what this community can offer you?

_____

_____

_____

_____

_____

_____

_____

_____

_____

_____

_____

_____

Glossary

What follows are three kinds of glossaries. There are as follows:

A General Glossary

Upland Specific Glossary – to help you understand terms you may come across in playing the game, and

The Ever-Changing Metaverse Glossary - terms that were added after we wrote the book in 2022. It is to help you quickly define new terms that can guide you to better understand what people are talking about as it relates to the game.

General Glossary

2FA - Two Factor Authentication - Using two devices to verify your identity while logging in to an app or website.

AMA - The acronym "AMA" means "ask me anything," and it's commonly used on social media sites. An AMA is a type of informal interview in which the interviewee is open to questions from the public.

Blockchain - A blockchain is a distributed ledger with growing lists of records (blocks) that are securely linked together via cryptographic hashes.

Cross Chain - This is in regard to moving assets from one blockchain or another or interacting with different blockchains.

DAPP - dApps have been developed to decentralize and disintermediate a range of functions and applications. These include things from self-executing financial contracts to multi-user games.

Decentralized - Having much of the decision-making power vested in teams, divisions, or local branches instead of in a single center of power.

DAO - A decentralized autonomous organization, a type of bottom-up entity structure with no central authority. Members of a DAO own tokens of the DAO, and members can vote on initiatives,

EOS - A blockchain platform for the development of decentralized applications (dApps). It makes dapp development easy by providing an operating-system-like set of services and functions that dapps can make use of. The idea behind EOS is to bring together the best features and promises of the various smart contract technologies out there (e.g., security of Bitcoin, computing support of Ethereum). Simply put, the EOS community is working to provide one simple to use, massively scalable dapp platform for the everyday user

KYC (Know Your Customer) - A legal requirement for financial institutions and financial services companies to establish a customer's identity and identify risk factors. KYC procedures help prevent identity theft, money laundering, financial fraud, terrorism financing, and other financial crimes.

Layer(s) - (Upland used as example)

Layer 0 - Blockchain (e.g., EOS)

Layer 1 - (e.g., Upland)

Layer 2 - (WOF, UPX world)

Mocaverse - The Mocaverse NFT collection represents the shared values and ethos of Animoca Brands and its portfolio companies and partners.

NFT (Non-Fungible Token) - It is a digital asset that can come in the form of art, music, in-game items, videos, and more. They are bought and sold online, frequently with cryptocurrency, and they are generally encoded with the same underlying software as many cryptos.

Node(Crypto) - A node, in the world of digital currency, is a computer that connects to a cryptocurrency network. The node or computer supports the network. It supports it through validation and relaying transactions. At the same time, it also gets a copy of the full blockchain. Any computer that connects to the Bitcoin network, for example, is a node.

OMA3 (OMA3™) - A collaboration of Web3 metaverse platform creators. Our goal is to ensure virtual land, digital assets, ideas, and services are highly interoperable between platforms and transparent to all communities.

Private Keys - The secret part of an asymmetric key pair that is typically used to digitally sign or decrypt data. A mathematical key (kept secret by the holder) used to create digital signatures and, depending upon the algorithm, to decrypt messages or files encrypted (for confidentiality) with the corresponding public key.

Public Keys - Used to verify a transaction after a transaction has been requested. Commonly a public key is also translated as an 'address' to receive cryptocurrencies. Whereas a private key that is associated with a cryptocurrency account focuses on authorizing the transaction.

Tilia - Company who provides USD processing for Upland and others.

UGC (User Generated Content) - Game assets created by players or users of a particular game or dApp.

Wallet - Crypto wallets keep your private keys - the passwords that give you access to your cryptocurrencies - safe and accessible, allowing you to send and receive cryptocurrencies like Bitcoin and Ethereum. They come in many forms, from hardware wallets (which looks like a USB stick) to mobile apps which are applications.

WAX - Decentralized platform for video game virtual asset trading, namely focused on the P2E and wider NFT space. The WAX blockchain has the potential to be a revolution in the gaming industry, ultimately making video games more affordable to the general public.

Web3 - Next iteration of the internet replacing "Big Tech" with decentralized organizations and blockchain technologies.

Upland Specific Glossary

As things are constantly in motion at Upland if any of the words below need updating, please let us know. Thank you.

3D Objects - These can be structures, vehicles, ornaments, outdoor decor, and other future items/assets. All properties yield 17.3% (per year, not month) that has now moved down to 14.7% when they are originally minted. If you buy on the secondary market, consider the original cost to mint the property.

Alcatraz - Uplands form of jail. Based on the infamous closed/retired Jail Island off the coast of San Francisco

Apartment Structure - Spark hours needed: 5800.

Assets - These are the digital items owned in the game.

Auctions - Usually done live on YouTube these are special sales for landmark properties or sometimes others that are performed by the Upland team live.

Banned - A player can get "banned" from the Official Discord server for different offenses. There are other ways to stay updated on the news of the game through the website and other Upland related Discord servers(see classified section) although being banned does hamper the ability for community involvement.

Beta - A working but unfinished version.

Block Explorers - This is your "avatar" or game piece (think monopoly) this is what represents you in the game.

Build - This is done with Spark in Upland. You can build structures on a property you own.

Chat - In game communication is located in lower left corner of screen-thought bubble icon.

Chief Executive Level Status - Net worth over 100 million.

City Releases - This is arguably one of the most exciting aspects of Upland when new cities are released, and it is a sort of race to get the most desired properties. It is a mixture of luck and skills to be successful during a new city release.

Collection Swap - Each collection in the game of Upland comes with a reward for obtaining it. These rewards increase with the rarity of the collection. There is a strategy where players can "swap" a collection with another player to collect the reward and then return the collection properties to the original owner. This led to a whole side economy in upland where players would do 50/50 swaps wherein the player loaning the collection would receive 50% of the reward from the players, they were loaning them to.

Competitive Hunt - A competitive hunt pits players against each other searching for the same treasures. These have a higher payout than the standard chests and are intermittently released/announced throughout the day with a 5:00 minute warning timer. There are different levels of competitive hunts with greater/lesser rewards.

Community Pool - Started with 50 billion UPX, when a player purchases UPX, they can now mint properties or other assets in the game. These purchases are paid into the community pool. All of the property yields and rewards (such as collection bonuses, treasure hunting rewards, etc.) are paid out to the players from this pool. If you purchase/sell assets on the secondary market (from another player), each player pays a 5% fee to the community pool. If the asset is sold in USD, the 5% USD fee is paid to Uplandme Inc. and the UPX equivalent is deposited to the community pool from the Upland pool.

Contribute Spark - Players can contribute spark to other players' builds by clicking on the players property>more>contribute.

Custom Model - When you reach Executive status (10,000,000 UPX net worth) you can request a custom model created just for you. This 3D Outdoor Decor object can be placed on one of your Upland properties.

Dark Blue Property Color – Property owned by you.

Dark Green Property Color – Property owned by another player and is listed for sale on the secondary market.

Delete Account - This is an option in the menu within the game. It will completely delete your account and prevent you from gaining access to your account. The upland team sends an email to verify you want to delete your account.

Director Block Explorer - This is the one of one Block Explorer Upland rewards its players with once they reach "Director" status(1 million net worth) You can obtain this by visiting "City Hall" in the game via your Block Explorer.

Director Level Status – Net worth over 1 million.

Enhanced Graphics - This is an option for how you view the game with your device.

Escrow - When a player puts an offer on another players property the offered amount will be put into ESCROW where money is held by a third party on behalf of two other parties that are in the process of completing a transaction.

Essentials - Most common base level version of sports collectibles in Upland.

Exclusive Collection - Orange - avg multiplier - 2.22%

Executive Level Status – Net worth over 10 million.

Factories - This is where in game products/assets are created using spark some of it created by players. They come in Small, Medium, and Large currently - each size has a different cost to build in spark hours relative to its size and the number of items it can produce each month.

Fan Points - These are allocated to the legits you own. Fan points have bonus benefits like first access to signatures, payouts etc.

Fees/Costs - All types and percentages. There are many types of fees. Send fees, community pool fees, upland fees, fees to convert UPX to USD.

Fiat - Currency usually paper or coin think Dollars, Euro, Pound, Yen etc.

Flipping - Term for buying and selling properties hopefully at a profit. Buy high, sell low! Just like in the real world buying something for one price and either by marketing, improvement or just time…. selling it for an increase.

Floating - This is what your Block Explorer does above the Upland Metaverse. This may change in the future but currently we are all just floating around.

Floor Price - After a city or neighborhood is fully minted(sold out) the "floor" is the lowest priced property in that area.

FSA (Fair Start Act) - Designed for players that have a total net worth under 100,000 Net Worth. The act allows players to purchase properties designated on the map on properties with the text "FSA" on them. Players above 100,000k Net Worth cannot purchase FSA properties.

Fuel for Vehicles - Currently none but will be spark in the future.

Game Ball - One of a kind for each NFL game played. You must be at the Stadium to purchase.

Genesis Week - This is a week celebrating the creation of Upland marked by events in the game and real life.

Genesis Property/City - The Genesis property or first city that was available to buy property in was San Francisco, The Genesis property was minted June 6th, 2019, by the Upland team and is the only property with 0 mint and 0 monthly interest. The current owner of this property is ThankMeLater.

Great Start - Measures the Visitor who had the most unique sends to their properties.

Grey (also spelled gray) Property Color – a property that has not been minted.

Home Address - You need to build a structure on your property to register a home address. Players with a home address are eligible to vote and it carries others perks for the neighborhood you reside in.

International Terminal - Refers to an airport terminal. It functions the same way as a terminal and as it is international, you can travel between countries.

In-Game Name (IGN) - References the name people go by when they joined Upland. This name cannot be changed.

Invite Referral - Link to join Upland - if used a bonus of 50% of new one-time purchase to the new user who used the code and 25% of that amount goes to the player who provided the link.

Jailed - If a player is "Jailed" their block explorer will be located in Alcatraz floating above that island outside of San Francisco.

Landmarks - These are real life properties that are reserved for special sale in the Upland metaverse.

Layer 2 - Other applications or games built on top of Upland(or another Layer 1 game/app).

Leaders - Option in "quick menu" in the game. Has leaderboards for competitions including completed collections - uplanders referred - treasures claimed - total UPX proceeds - trades.

Legits - Sports cards generally speaking.

Levels/Status - The game of Upland has different names for players at different levels in the game as follows, Uplander, Pro, Director, Executive, and Chief Executive. Each level indicates a minimum net worth. For example, Uplander level status indicates a minimum net worth of 10,000.

Light Blue Property Color – Property that is owned by another player and is not listed for sale on the secondary market.

Light Green Property Color – Property that is available to be minted. *If it says FSA, only Uplanders and Visitors are able to mint it.

Limited Collection - Purple - avg multiplier - 1.77%.

Luxury Modern House Structure - Spark hours: 3000.

Mascot - The Upland metaverse mascot is a llama named Miles.

Minting - This is describing the initial purchase of a property or other asset. Assets can be bought and sold after minting but that first purchase is the only one of those transactions that is considered and referred to as "minting".

Metaventures - These are player owned and operated businesses within the Upland metaverse.

Metaventure Dues - These are the monthly amount the business owner pays for their store. Amounts are based on the city and neighborhood and some other factors.

Metaventure Fees - These are fees that the shop owner charges to buy and sell from their shop. These can be up to 6% and are added to the 5% fees that Upland charges.

Micro House Structure - Spark hours: 500.

Momentos - Type of legit - most Rare - NFL versions are 1 of 1's, FIFA can range from 1of1's to 1 out of 60, these have more fan points.

Monthly Earnings - Is the ROI (return on investment) for owning properties in Upland.

MV- Motors Cars - The first car brand to enter the Metaverse is Upland's MV-Motors. These cars are produced at 4220 Network Circle in Santa Clara, California. Cars will be required not only for racing and delivering goods but also for traveling within a city.

Neighborhood - Each city is divided up into separate neighborhoods. These are delineated and named in the Upland Metaverse, you can toggle this view by clicking the pin on the lower right side of the screen.

Net Worth - Total combination of property value and UPX in a player's account. Does not include other in game assets such as block explorers, legits, ornaments and structures which may add more potential value to an account.

Node - A neighborhood or street where players have connected and converged to build and develop as a group.

Operator - Development team that runs Upland (currently Upland me inc.).

Outdoor Decor- 3D models that can be arranged on a player's properties.

Ownership Celebrations - These occur when a player mints a property, a screen pops up and confetti flies and a globe with text saying "you are the owner" pops up. This is an option in settings that you can turn off or on(if you are trying to mint a new city this can definitely slow you down so you may want to turn this item off during releases.

People's Champ - Measures the number of unique sends by a Player to Visitor properties.

Pools - The pools are what hold the fees collected.

Portal - This a function of the game where you can import NFT's from outside of Upland into the game of Upland.

Pro Level Status – Net worth over 100,000.

Profile Picture - You can choose a block explorer and a city/neighborhood and then you can download an image with that information on it.

Properties - These are real life addresses in both Upland and the real world.

Property Collections - These are group properties that have a monthly earning multiplier. There are different levels of collection: Standard, limited, exclusive, rare, and Ultra Rare. Each has an average monthly multiplier increase.

Pickup Trucks - - Type of vehicle available in the Upland Game.

Property Colors - Properties are assigned colors that have special meaning during a city release and beyond. The colors include, grey (gray), light green, light blue, dark green.

Race Cars - Type of vehicle available in the Upland Game.

Racing - Game function in Upland where you can utilize your in-game vehicles.

Ranch House Structure - Spark hours: 1100

Rare Collection - Red- avg multiplier - 2.52%.

Rising Star - Measures the Player who completes the most collections during the week.

Sedans - Type of vehicle available in the Upland Game.

Sales Fees - When buying and selling properties each player is charged 5% of the total amount is charged in addition to each of the players resulting in a 10% fee total.(for example if Joe buys a property for 1000 UPX from Olivia he will be charged 1050 and she will receive 950.).

Secondary Market - Properties that have been purchased/minted and put back on the open market for sale.

Semi Trucks with Trailers - Type of vehicle available in the Upland Game.

Send Fees - These range in amount by city. These can be set individually or as a group of all properties owned within a city by clicking on the three dots on the top right of the property card.

Sends - You need these to move from place to place in Upland. The max you can get by collecting them(paper airplanes in game) is 11. Each day at 4 PM PST.

Showrooms - This is where you send the items created in your factories to show and sell to the community. These also come in Small, Medium and Large currently - each size has a different cost to build in spark hours relative to its size and the number of items it can hold in inventory. There are also landmarks and stadiums that have and will be produced. There are also an array of city specific buildings that were created by Upland Users.

Small Town House Structure (Flat Roof)- Spark hours: 950.

Small Town House Structure (Slope Roof) - Spark hours: 950

Spark - Allows players to build/create in-game items, such as structures.

Spark Hours - 1 spark hour equals 1 spark being used for 60 minutes. If you had only .5 spark to use, then 1 spark hour would equal 120 minutes.

Spark Week - This is usually once a month and spark sales and contests happen as well as a higher reward for leveling up your status during those periods.

Spud - This was the precursor to Spark. There were building competitions called the Spud wars, but all the structures were removed after the competition/test.

Structures - There are different types of structures that can be built, and each requires a certain number of spark hours to

Structure Ornament - These are Upland, and player created designs that go over your structure to give it a new look. Mainly used during holidays etc.

Standard Challenges - Usually held monthly or bimonthly.

Standard Collection – Blue - avg multiplier - 1.33%.

Standard Hunt - These are solo hunts which can be spawned 24/7. You can earn UPX and Spark and help train for competitive hunts against other players with greater rewards.

Stem - Very similar to Spark in that it allows players to build/create in game items. The difference is Spark allows players to create physical material inanimate objects, while Stem allows players to create/build living items such as plants and animals.

Strategy- Just like life, everyone has a different strategy on the best way to play. Most of the best players continuously modify that strategy as the game progresses cand changes.

Street View - This is an option on all properties in Upland. It is connected to google earth so you can explore the properties, games/web services there is a support team who responds to questions and emails. Also, you can reach out in the support channel in the official upland server.

SUVs - Type of vehicle available in the Upland Game.

Tagged Marketplace Markers - Some properties have "tags" or marketplace markers.

Transfer Fees - When transferring UPX to another player 5% of the total amount is charged in addition to each of the players resulting in a 10% fee total.(for example if Joe sends 1000 UPX to Olivia he will be charged 1050 and she will receive 950.).

Travel - Planes, trains, buses and even the Hyperlink(between Chicago and Cleveland) are all ways to travel in Upland. The developers try to mirror the real world in some respects and this is one, and although you won't need to Uber to the terminal and check in your bags but you will need to send your block explorer to the airport and purchase a ticket and wait the amount of travel time before arriving at your destination.

Treasure Hunting - This is a mini game within upland where you search for a "treasure" by traveling around upland looking at directional arrow clues trying to locate a treasure chest or Pinata which gives the finder UPX or Spark prizes.

Treasure Rush - In this mode, Uplanders are challenged to spawn and collect as many treasures as possible in the 15 (30) minute period; no sends will be consumed while hunting. The more Treasures you find, the higher you will place on each City's leaderboard.

Treasure Web - In a strategy to conserve sends and the cost of send fees during a hunt some players will build "treasure webs" which are evenly distanced properties within a city so they can send to their own properties during hunts which cost 0 fees band 0 sends.

UGC (User Generated Content) - In game assets created by players.

Ultra Rare Collection - Yellow - avg multiplier - 2.77%.

UPLAND - A blockchain-based Metaverse game, with NFT real estate allowing earnings from buying and selling virtual properties.

Upland's City Hall - Located in San Francisco – the first city in the Upland Metaverse. The City Hall serves a number of important functions, possibly more in the future. The location of Upland's City Hall is: 1 Dr. Carlton B Goodlet Place, San Francisco CA

Uplander Level Status - Minimum net worth of 10,000.

Upland Pool - Started with 50 billion UPX. The Upland pool exists to fuel in-game activities and fund operator (Uplandme Inc. -the company behind Upland) development.

UPX - This is the in-game currency for upland. It has traditionally and currently been sold for 1000 per US Dollar.

UPX Transfer - This is an in-game function where one player can send UPX directly to another by accessing the plates profile by either searching in the search player tool or by clicking on the name when seen. On each player's profile card there is a link that says " send UPX" you click it and follow instructions.****Before a player can send UPX it must be in their account for over 60 days. This time resets if a player purchases new UPX through the store during the 60-day period.

USD (United States Dollar) – United States monetary currency.

Utility - The ability to use or utilize your digital assets.

Vans - Type of vehicle available in the Upland Game.

Vanilla Release - This is a type of new city release where the collections are/are not announced prior to the release date. Collections are usually revealed about one to two weeks after the release and speculation and sales are high during this period.

Vehicles - There are vehicles in the game of Upland for shipping digital assets and to move players around the metaverse and for racing. There are currently types of vehicles in Upland are semi-trucks with trailers, pickup trucks, vans, sedans, and SUVs.

WOF (World of Futbol) - The first official layer 2 game implemented in the Upland metaverse. There are stadiums built in different cities where you can click on them and see a button that links you to this separate game through Upland.

The Ever-Changing Metaverse Glossary

The topics below give a brief description of changes that have occurred in Upland over the period of June 2022 through July 2023. They cover the following eight categories. Partnerships, Player Run Businesses, Communication/Community Building, Cities Launched, Travel, Layer 2/Gaming, Genesis 2023 Award Winners and General (for milestones that occurred not mentioned in other categories).

<u>Partnerships</u>: Upland formed partnerships with the following companies. The order is based on the approximate month/quarter of the year that the partnership was announced. All of these partnerships encourage bridge building with other niche communities for sports fans, charities, other gamers, artists and more to increase the size and scope of the metaverse helping transcend borders and cultures creating a global community.

June 2022 - New partnership with, FC Porto, the #1 Futbol/Soccer team in Portugal who won the 2022 Primeira Liga Championship.

Oct 2022 - Upland & Gala Games Partner Up. The goal of the partnership is to add value to digital assets and create new dynamic experiences for players.

Oct 2022 - Jacky Tsai (Contemporary Artist) adds the MetaSkull Collection.

Oct 2022 - Susan G. Komen® and Upland Partner in the Fight against Breast Cancer. It is just one more demonstration of how the Upland community comes together.

Nov 2022 - Upland and FIFA officially launched the FIFA World Cup Qatar 2022 experience in Upland's metaverse.

Dec 2022 - Long-term partnership with UNICEF Brazil. Another charity that the community supports.

April 2023 - Upland's exclusive partnership with the Argentina Football Association (AFA). Upland is the only place fans can own video highlights of Argentina's biggest football moments.

May 2023 - The Stock Car Pro Series Brazil partnered with Upland to bring professional racing to the Metaverse.

May 2023 - Upland has partnered with NOWHERE to launch the first immersive 3D experiences called, "Cafes." Using NOWHERE's technology, players are able to socialize with spatial audio, share screens or live stream, play games, and show off their 3D avatars.

UGC (User Generated Content): Upland is one of the few Metaverse games to allow users/players to create assets (their own in-game items) within the game.

July 2022 - Player designed racetracks.

Aug 2022 - Upland Designers Guild - Assist players in creating a variety of assets like ornaments, chairs, flags, buildings, Go Karts, etc. for Upland.

Dec 2022 - Carnaval Ornament Contest - Players were invited to design and submit their own custom 3D Structure Ornament models.

June 2023 - Player designed and manufactured Go Karts

June 2023 - In the weeks following Genesis Week, Metaventure applications opened for players to apply for their own manufacturing plant to later design and build their own creative and unique Go Karts.

Player Run Businesses: Upland allows its players to more than just play the game. It offers them a way to create a business. These can be located as orange dots on the Upland Map.

July 2022 -Uplanders could begin construction on their own Factory, which powers the manufacturing of all 3D objects in the Upland metaverse.

Aug 2022 - Block Explorer Shops & NFLPA Fan Shops. Players are able to apply for a Metaventure at any time.

Sept 2022 - Players as part of the Outdoor Decor Beta can begin manufacturing their own outdoor decor items.

Sept 2022 - Showrooms are now available! These unique structures are integral to the future of Upland as they will allow Uplanders to sell 3D items, such as Outdoor Decor(also known as Map Assets) and other assets in the Metaverse.

Oct 2022 - Players can shop for Outdoor Decor (also known as Map Assets) in player-run showrooms.

Oct 2022 - Car Showroom Metaventures and the long-anticipated new larger structures that allow players to sell cars are here.

Feb 2023 - Players could apply for a Structure Ornament Showroom or Factory (or both).

June 2023 – Player-run Business booths at Genesis week. Exhibitors had booths to showcase their Upland projects to the community.

Communication/Community Building: Developing community is a key element of the game and the mission of the company. The items listed below are some of the improvements and tools that help with that mission.

Aug 2022 - Introducing a new UPX funding mechanism for the Upland Pool and the first-ever, in-game economic ballot.

Dec 2022 - In-Game Chat is Finally Here

Apr 2023 - Neighborhood Ratings arrived with competitions rewarding top-performing Nodes with new Neighborhood Collections!

May 2023 - Upland Launched the first immersive 3D experiences called Cafes.

June 2023 - Mission Center, created to guide and reward new players through their Upland journey.

June 2023 - Gaia, has joined Miles the Llama as Upland's official mascot.

Cities Launched: As the Metaverse grows, more and more cities open up. The cities added as of July 2022 to the game include:

July/2022 - Rio De Janeiro- Brazil,
Aug 2022 - Porto- Portugal,
Sept 2022 - Dallas and Arlington, Texas are coming to the Metaverse,
Jan 2023 - Buenos Aires- Argentina,
Feb 2023 - Sao Paulo - Brazil
Apr 2023 - London and Birmingham - England
June 2023 - Berlin - Germany

Travel: Upland tries to replicate the real world in options for travel. Traveling by car was added (although not officially functioning yet) to the other options already in place: plane, train, bus. More options and improvements to unfold.

MV Motors Car sales have occurred many times over this period and continue sporadically.

Layer2/Gaming: Upland is a "Layer 1" game (see glossary) and it allows other game developers to launch with their game/metaverse on top of it in "Layer 2.". Examples below:

Sept 2022 - Community Development Tools introduced, where developers can connect their third-party experiences to the Upland platform. These are found as purple dots on the Upland map.

List of Layer 2 games/applications (look for purple dots) on Upland:

Upland Spark Exchange - A place for people to rent or lease Spark for building assets within Upland.

The Real Node LA - Mall/Gallery/School - Set in the application Spatial connect through Upland to this coinciding Metaverse.

WOF- World of Futbol - A Soccer Futbol game where players can wager UPX in head-to-head gameplay.

Upland Kingdoms - Is a new game from the Upland Developers Network where you play as a medieval lord with your realm being the properties that you own in Upland! Your job will be to turn the wilderness into a thriving fiefdom.

Uplandia - Presents players with a series of quests and challenges, each offering its own set of objectives and rewards. These quests can take players on virtual journeys through intricate storylines, requiring strategic thinking, problem-solving skills, and collaboration with other players to complete.

Taco Tools -An application that unlocks hidden items and information within the Upland metaverse, offering players a deeper understanding of the game and enabling them to optimize their gameplay experience. From revealing send fees to providing additional features and fostering a supportive community.

Ladiez MetaSoccer - Winner of the 2023 Hackathon. A multiplayer women's soccer game created in honor of the FIFA Women's World Cup 2023™. Promoting diversity, inclusivity, and utility for FIFA Legits in Upland

The X - The X Range is an engaging weapons training range offering players the choice to compete in either an intense 1v1 showdown or tournament mode, with the opportunity to play for UPX.

Genesis Week Community Award Winners: Upland's Genesis Week 2023 was held in person in Las Vegas at the Sahara hotel. During the event, awards and prizes were given out. It is an informative and fun event that is of benefit players to attend, if at all possible. Congratulations to all the winners.

Player of the Year: Shaktilyn
Designer of the Year: Antikmaster
Broadcaster of the Year: YK2012

Hackathon Project Winners: A hackathon is an event where developers, designers, artists, gamers enthusiasts come together to collaborate and create innovative games and experiences. The goal is to empower developers by equipping them with the tools, support, and inspiration needed to build revolutionary games and experiences within the Upland metaverse.

The project winners were as follows:

FIFA Track: FIFA Fantasy League by Hacker and Ikris
Innovation Track: Block Raiders by Desjaak and Team
FIFA Design Challenge: Around the World by Deathender

<u>General</u>: Below are items that did not fit into the above categories yet deserve to be mentioned.

Jan 2023 - Upland players are crossing perhaps the most impressive and meaningful milestone in metaverse history: they're breaking the $10 million mark in NFT-to-USD!

Feb 2023 - Players can go into their Upland Profile and build a new 3D Avatar. These avatars will be used to access 3D experiences connected to Upland.

March 2023 - Lost properties offer players a unique opportunity to own fantastic locations in some of the metaverse's most highly sought cities!

The Upland team has gotten better at mapping Upland cities to real-world city grids. This means we have been able to map properties that were originally missed at city openings. During this Lost Properties Sale, properties were released that were not opened for minting during the initial city launch.

UPLAND Bureau created -When a lost property becomes available, it will be sold by the Upland Bureau on the secondary market. These properties will be minted by the Upland Bureau at their original base mint price, but after minting, these properties will be listed for sale, at current market value, for players to purchase.

Apr 2023 - Uncollected earnings cap - UPX earnings for owned properties in Upland. This new feature requires players to login and collect their property earnings before hitting a certain cap.

Apr 2023 - Wearables (AKA Fashion) were introduced. Wearables are a type of Legit(NFT) players can use to customize their 3D Avatars.

(In Process) Preparing for the introduction of Life, which will be powered by the STEM token.

July 2023 - Upland opened an NFT asset portal to Ethereum. With this integration, Uplanders are able to leverage the power of Ethereum for their Upland assets starting with Block Explorers

Classifieds

The classified section that follows list Upland related content such as metaventure stores, podcasts, as well as web addresses, Discord contact information, or emails as well content related to books, and services offered by members of the community. It is arranged in alphabetical order and include only members that have been interviewed in this book.

Introduction to Classifieds

The classifieds below are arranged in alphabetical order by the in-name game of the person whose essay you read in the Interviews section.

BEN68
Samurai Aquatics -
https://discord.gg/CPpMk8mPfF

MetaverseVenturesEntertainment
https://www.youtube.com/@MetaverseVenturesEntertainment

BLEURAIN
https://youtube.com/@zarinahsguides4686

CAFE MORGADOR
Upland Daily Server
https://discord.gg/nzhxxVM4GK

CMAVS
DRL: Detroit Rally League
An auto racing association based in Detroit Motor City.
https://discord.gg/sgP52JqWw4

Victory Motors
A Vehicle Design and Manufacturing Showroom
Company focus is on motorsports racing. Showroom at 22330 Victory Blvd. LA
https://discord.gg/EVtHteQCre

Alcove Ent.
An entertainment company developing games and experiences in Upland.
https://discord.gg/x6FPeNkFyj

MCAAD: Motor City Automotive Arts District
A racing and car culture community located in Gratiot Town Detroit.
https://discord.gg/krPnNeyR3a

CARZ
A racers group developing race zone communities in Arlington Texas.
https://discord.gg/fGjDeea2th

Berkeley Hills
A community node in the SF Bay Area.
https://discord.gg/gDgGv7QDBq

DAK
Perpetual Good in the Metaverse
https://tinyurl.com/bdff8fv5

DEATHENDER
https://linktr.ee/detech

DESJAAK
The Analytic Assassins Discord server.
https://discord.gg/gQeJ5WAN2K

Discord invite to The Donut: Upland Creator Society
https://discord.gg/4pYB6mtBJJ   -

All Design and Projects by DeSjaak
www.desjaakdesign.com

HACKER
UPXland.me

HUMANSIMULATION
Upland Minting Guides by Humansim | Bananastim
Looking for help on where to buy property in one of the fastest growing

Upland Minting Guides - A website specialized in creating and distributing
minting guides for Upland City Releases
https://bit.ly/HSBS_UplandMintingGuides

HUMBLELIFE/CHET
Fiskhorn Community Discord
https://discord.gg/sVGTKAkh

JASMILLS
Century Nodes
https://discord.gg/Pwx2uXZkFT
https://twitter.com/CenturyCitizens

JOELIVES/JOE HERNANDEZ
https://4thwalldigital.com
https://mobile.twitter.com/Acrylicks
https://www.instagram.com/4thwalldigital/

KCBC
Uplando's Discord Channel

LAKEGIRL/TAMMY
www.thetrueairhead.com

MORCHEESE/ANGELA
MVE - Metaverse Ventures Entertainment
https://discord.gg/NPGMPNwmED
https://mve.productions/

Art for the Whine and Cheese show:
https://www.morecheezwax.com/

MUCIDA
https://www.youtube.com/c/upland_brasil
Instagram: https://www.instagram.com/upland_brasil/
telegram: https://t.me/uplandbr

SATOSHISVIEW
https://linktr.ee/satoshisview

SHAKTILYN
Ave of Fashion - A channel in the server below
https://discord.gg/NevNe54pRg

Creedmore Hub
https://discord.gg/44Wp4QDRsV

TDAVIS/TD
Crypto News, Games, Reviews, Drop Schedules, Live Streams
https://dsc.gg/nftg
https://nftg.tv/
NFT/De-Fi/Crypto

THANKMELATER
UPX.World - A web3 Layer 2 Gaming Platform for Upland and beyond.

UMBRELLA BOY
https://twitter.com/_umbrellaboy_

Meet the Upland Team

Meet the Co-Founders & Co-CEOs of Uplandme, Inc.

| Dirk Lueth | Idan Zukerman | Mani Honigstein |

Uplandme, Inc. has three founders. The me in Uplandme stands for metaverse. Upland is a location-based virtual property trading game people often describe it as kind of like Monopoly. They have chosen to use blockchain technology because they wanted to create a credible real-life economy that powers the game. An economy where people can enjoy the concept of true ownership. An economy where people are free to trade digital assets in the open market. An economy where people can liquidate their assets and exit the game if they choose to do so. An economy where all transactions are secured and transparent on the blockchain. Here is a very brief introduction to them. You can discover more about them on LinkedIn and many of the podcasts on YouTube about Upland.

Dirk Lueth. Co-Founder & Co-Ceo, Uplandme, Inc.

Dirk is originally from Germany and now lives in the United States. He has a PhD in Economics and plays a key role in developing the economics of the metaverse. After he finished his PhD, he had the choice to either go work for the European Central bank or for the Federal Reserve in the U.S. but since the age of 16 had an entrepreneurial spirit in him. In his heart he knew he enjoyed starting new projects and coming up with new concepts. When he was in Germany, he started two companies and that was where he got his introduction into blockchain. He is the leader of OMA3 a group which is setting the standards for the future Metaverse.

Idan Zukerman. Co-Founder & Co-CEO, Uplandme, Inc.

Idan, was a part of the founding team of a company called *RocketPlay* which built a successful social casino game called *Lucky Play Casino*, it eventually got acquired. In 2015 he became more and more aware of blockchain technology, but it wasn't until the coming out of the Ethereum blockchain and other subsequent innovation that took place that he started to get excited about what this technology could mean for the gaming space. Fast forward to the coming out of the EOS blockchain he went on a mission to bring the benefits of blockchain technology to mass audiences through gaming.

Mani Honigstein, Co-Founder of Uplandme, Inc.

Mani is a tech investor. He was a past Co-founder & CEO at *RocketPlay*. He is a Managing Partner at Honeystone Ventures, Investor at Zeotap, as well as a Co-founder at Upland.

David Paskett, Upland's Head of Community

The Upland Metaverse is a digital world where people can interact and connect in new and exciting ways. It is a world where we can come together as a community, sharing our experiences, and establishing meaningful relationships with each other. Ultimately, Upland's community is a testament to the strength of human connection.

As Upland's Head of Community, I have experienced this power of community firsthand, and it has been a positive, challenging, and unique experience.

It is my responsibility, as well as that of my team, to foster a sense of belonging and community among Uplanders. To achieve this, players are actively encouraged to interact with each other and given the opportunity to connect through events, chat, or other activities. In order to ensure everyone feels safe and respected, it is also essential to set clear rules for behavior and enforce them whenever necessary.

Being a voice for the community and advocating for their needs has also been an honor, whether through direct engagement with Upland developers or collaboration with other Upland players.

Anyone who plays Upland knows that we are not alone. In this world, we can come together to share our passions, collaborate on projects, and offer support to one another, each with their own unique stories, perspectives, and experiences. This sense of community allows us to express our true selves, free of the constraints of our physical surroundings.

Through this connection, Upland has the power to heal and inspire us. When we are feeling lonely or disconnected, we can find comfort in this virtual community, where people from all over the world are just a message away. Likewise, we can also bond over our shared interests and hobbies.

Upland has the potential to connect people in ways previously unimaginable if we do our job correctly.

It is still the early days in Upland, but the strength of community is a testament to how human connection thrives, even in a digital world. Upland has served as a place for players to get together, share experiences, and support one another, and I have had the privilege of witnessing that connection firsthand.

As we continue to build Upland, let us remember that we are not alone, and that the community will always be there to bring us together.

Meet the Authors

About Olivia Whiteman

Olivia Whiteman is a rising star in the field of productivity and work-life harmony, driven by her personal journey of transformation. After a life-altering accident forced her to reimagine her path, she became determined to find a way to navigate stress, overwhelm, and the pressures of unfinished tasks. Through her own experience, she developed a powerful system, "Turbocharge Your Results," that not only helped her regain control but also allowed her to thrive in all aspects of life.

With her firsthand understanding and perspective of the challenges faced by professionals, Olivia is on a mission to share her system and help others to reach their true potential.

Olivia places a special emphasis on working with upper-level management, recognizing that a positive work culture and effective leadership at the top have a profound ripple effect throughout an organization. By implementing her Turbocharge system, leaders can not only optimize their own productivity but also inspire and empower their teams to thrive.

With a focus on achieving work-life harmony and finding time for what truly matters, Olivia offers a refreshing and practical approach to transforming the way we work and live.

Olivia offers a fresh perspective and actionable strategies to cultivate a more productive, balanced, and engaged workforce. Her presentations and interactive workshops helps leaders create greater success, fulfillment, and inspire positive change.

Olivia is also an accomplished writer and creator of transformational resources. With a passion for personal development, creativity, and productivity, she has produced or participated in several compilation book that explore a wide range of topics, empowering readers to unlock their potential and live fulfilling lives. Several of these books have been granted Amazon #1 Best Seller status.

About Joe Hernandez

Artist, educator, grandfather and now author. After spending many years in corporate construction, building prisons, schools, and highways all over the Southern California area, Joe received his Masters Degree in Fine Art and studied finance at the prestigious Peter F. Drucker School of Business. He has taught at universities and high schools throughout the Southern California area.

A lover of fun, Joe, has designed and built art and lightning installations for concerts, festivals, and events worldwide. In 2015, he was in an accident which left him paralyzed from the neck down. After being told he would never have the use of his arms or legs again, he miraculously recovered and cherishes every day where he can walk and use his hands to do good in the world.

Your Turn

Be In Our Next Book

We had so much fun creating this book. We are already considering creating a second version. If you are interested in being included in this second book, send your submission to ouruplandbook@gmail.com.

First time submitters, please answer the following questions:

What is your IGN (in-game name)?

When did you join Upland and who introduced you?

How do you plan to serve or want to be recognized in the community?

Why did you join Upland and what do you think is in its future?

If you have submitted an entry before, please answer the following questions:

What is your IGN (in-game name)?

Please share a highlight from being part of the Upland community since your last submission.

Please share a connection you have made through Upland, and its benefit to you.

What additions to the game would you like to see?